D1259742

THE EAGLE'S WORD

ALSO BY GERALD VANN

ON BEING HUMAN · MORALS AND MAN

MORALITY AND WAR · OF HIS FULLNESS

ST THOMAS AQUINAS · THE HEART OF MAN

THE DIVINE PITY · HIS WILL IS OUR PEACE

EVE AND THE GRYPHON · THE PAIN OF CHRIST

AWAKE IN HEAVEN · THE TWO TREES

THE SEVEN SWORDS · THE HIGH GREEN HILL

THE WATER AND THE FIRE · THE PARADISE TREE

TO HEAVEN WITH DIANA

IN COLLABORATION WITH P. K. MEAGHER, O.P.

STONES OR BREAD?

THE
EAGLE'S WORD

A PRESENTATION OF THE

GOSPEL ACCORDING TO ST JOHN

WITH AN INTRODUCTORY ESSAY BY

GERALD VANN, O.P.

A HELEN AND KURT WOLFF BOOK

HARCOURT, BRACE & WORLD, INC., NEW YORK

LEO DEHON LIBRARY
P.O. BOX 429
226.26
V334
HALES CORNERS, WI 53130-0429

ST. JOSEPH'S NOVITIATE
BAILEYS HARBOR, WISCONSIN

© 1961 by Gerald Vann, O.P.
All rights reserved. No part of this book may be reproduced in any
form or by any mechanical means, including mimeograph and
tape recorder, without permission in writing from the publisher.
first American edition

Imprimi Potest
Henricus St John, O.P.
Prior Provincialis
Londini die 11 Martii 1961

Nihil Obstat
Raymundus P. Redmond, S.T.D., Ph.D.
Censor Deputatus

Imprimatur
✠ Jacobus
Episcopus Hagulstadensis
et Novocastrensis

Novocastri die 21 Februarii 1961

Library of Congress Catalog Card Number: 61-15809
Printed in the United States of America

CONTENTS

INTRODUCTION

THE EAGLE'S WORD

ACKNOWLEDGEMENT

We are grateful to Messrs Faber for permission to include quotations from *Collected Poems 1909–1935* and *Four Quartets* by T. S. Eliot

INTRODUCTION

1. The Idiom of the Fourth Gospel

This book is not a new translation of the fourth gospel. Its purpose may perhaps be best explained by explaining its origin. Some time ago I was asked to write a paraphrase or adaptation of the prayers of the Mass in language which would be meaningful for children; and when I realized that this meant not only the prayers of the Canon but all the prayers which are said daily without change, my first reaction was to say that at least as far as the 'last gospel' (i.e. the prologue to *St John*) was concerned the task was an impossible one. However, having in the end been induced to attempt it, I at once found myself fascinated by the problems and challenges it involved; and then the thought struck me that it might be worth while attempting something of the sort, not just for children but for adults who are not biblical scholars, with the gospel as a whole: keeping as closely as possible to the text but at the same time adapting it where necessary by paraphrasing, expanding, re-arranging, in the hope of thus enabling the reader to follow St John's thought and to catch something of its richness and depth without having to refer constantly to commentaries and dictionaries.

Embarking on the task means, for one who is not a biblical scholar, discovering how little of the text one has hitherto really understood. There are pages we have read or listened to so often that we know them almost by heart, but we may have contented ourselves with grasping their general sense and then concentrating on their salient sentences or phrases, perhaps without ever realizing how much of the rest is unintelligible to us. To study the text in detail is to be forced again and again to admit that one does not really know what a given word or phrase means. What, for instance, did the risen Christ really say to Mary Magdalen in 20^{17}?[1] And incidentally, having 'turned round' and seen Jesus, in 20^{14}, how can she, in 20^{16}, turn to him again?[2] Or, while a given sentence is clear enough in itself, one will often find difficulty in seeing how it fits into the context (as in 12^{23}, where our Lord's words seem to ignore rather than to answer the disciples' message about the Greeks who wished to see him).[3]

Moreover one has constantly to ask, not merely what the exact meaning of a phrase is, but how *many* meanings it is intended to convey. The prophetic vision is many-levelled, mingling past or present with future, the temporal with the eternal, the literal with the metaphorical, history with symbol. It has been well said that in the fourth gospel there are no parables because the whole gospel is a parable: John is describing events which took place in historical time, but the events are themselves symbols, and therefore the narrative is concerned simultaneously with the historical happenings in the past and with their timeless significance for us here and now in the present. If we are told that water is drawn from a well or

[1] cf. *infra*, pp. 114–15.   [2] cf. *infra*, p. 98.   [3] cf. *infra*, pp. 84–6.

poured out for washing, that wine is drunk, that fish is caught and cooked, or bread broken and distributed, the account is not only a chronicling of facts but a communicating of vital truth. And when, for instance, we are told that 'blood and water' flowed from the side of the dead Christ, we are concerned far less with the chronicling than with the communicating, just as it is not for its historical importance but for its symbolical significance that the account of Christ's Passion is introduced, as Judas leaves the supper-table to sell his Master, with the words 'And it was night'.

We live out our mortal lives in joy and sadness, in failure and pathos but also in eagerness and expectancy, because life is a *chiaroscuro*, the light and shadow of a world fallen yet redeemed, a world in which evil conquers but is conquered. The evil is conquered because the Light came and 'lived for a time amongst us' and shone forth in our darkness, and 'the darkness could not master it'. The eternal Word is God's self-utterance; the incarnate Word is that utterance revealed, communicated, given to us in the person of Jesus. In the beginning God had said 'Let there be light'; and light was made, the first cosmic creature; but in the fullness of time, in the moment of cosmic renewal, the Light was given—and with their own eyes Christ's first followers saw the Glory clothed in human flesh. It is to this moment that all history leads; in Christ the whole cosmic process culminates and is 'summed up';[1] and while on the one hand the Light reveals to us the meaning of history, of process, of our

[1] *Ephes.* 1[10].

mundane reality, on the other hand it is through God's historical 'words'—through the events of history, especially the history of the Jewish people, and above all the history of the life and death of Jesus—that the meaning of the Word is revealed to us. Yet still we see only 'as in a glass, darkly': to say that the darkness cannot master the Light is to say both that the Light cannot be conquered and that it cannot be fully understood; Christ lives still in the midst of us, but it is in a hidden manner, like that in which he went up secretly to Jerusalem, and the search for him is a search in darkness, like that of Nicodemus who came to him secretly by night. By night because if darkness is the enemy, is evil and emptiness and the sterility into which Judas is plunged by denying the Light, it is also, like the dark waters of the primeval chaos, the womb from which light and life must spring, it is fertility, it is what it was for Peter in his sorrow, the promise and potentiality of glory, of transfiguration into the light of a new dawn.

To understand the fourth gospel it is not enough to know the dictionary-meaning of the words it contains: if its language is that of prophetic vision it is also that of poetic vision, and poetry is concerned with symbol and paradox and evocation. John tells us that the Word became human flesh and blood and 'lived for a time in the midst of us': but we shall miss a great deal of his thought unless we start from the literal meaning of the Greek, that the Word 'pitched his tent within our midst': in thus evoking the distant nomadic past of his people, John evokes both the transience and the intimacy of nomadic life, and the sense of intimacy is strengthened by the prepositional phrase, which almost means 'within us'; further, the idea of living in a tent (or being 'tabernacled') leads us straight back to the Old Testament, to the tabernacle which housed the ark of the covenant, the place where God's glory dwelt, the divine presence made visibly manifest in a 'pillar of cloud'; again, the Greek verb *skēnoun*, to live in a tent, recalls (not only by similarity of sense but by identity of consonants) the Hebrew word *Shekinah*, dwelling-place, and in the Old Testament the word is used to signify not only the place where God was present but also that presence itself, and its visible manifestation, the glory, so that finally it came to be used as a synonym for the Godhead itself. But for John the incarnate Word is himself the place and the visible manifestation of the divine presence and its glory; is indeed himself that infinite and uncreated Glory; for the *Logos*, the Word, is the Light: God's self-utterance is infinite radiance in the sense both of splendour and of a radiation of vitality and energy like that of the radiant sun—for the Son of God is the Sun of righteousness, of holiness, and *bonum est diffusivum sui*, it is of the nature of goodness, of love, to be outward-turning, to give life and splendour to others by the giving of itself.

Thus it was 'through the Word that all things were made: through him life is given to all that is': in the imagery of *Genesis* it was through him that the dark waters of formless chaos were transfigured and given the harmony and beauty of an ordered cosmos. And here we are reminded of the *Book of Wisdom*: if the Word of God is the Glory of God he is also the Wisdom of God, the 'pure effluence of his glory who is God all-powerful, . . . the glow that radiates from eternal light, . . . the untarnished mirror of God's majesty, . . . the faithful echo of his goodness', whose brightness is 'beyond the brightness of the sun and all the starry host'.[1]

To most readers today, *Logos* (Word) is not the familiar concept it was to those for whom John was immediately writing; and it may help us to understand the term as John uses it if we see it first of all as comprising the content of the two other terms, creative Wisdom and eternal Son: the Wisdom through whom not only the designing of all order and beauty but the carrying out of the design, the creating of the cosmos and the cosmic order, is achieved, for 'from the very beginning, mounted on the heaven of heavens, God utters his word in a voice of power' (cf. *Ps.* 67[34]); and the Son who receives all from the Father, yet is in all respects the equal of the Father, and is at the same time the Godhead's 'radiance', the Sun and the Glory.

It was this Glory which the disciples saw with their own eyes and touched with their hands; yet at the same time the Glory was within them: 'I live in my Father and you live in me and I in you' (14[20]): they were 'children

[1] *Wisd.* 7[25-9]. The fact that the scriptures here speak of Wisdom as feminine should save us from any danger of a too intellectual interpretation of such terms as *Logos* and Wisdom, and remind us that this Wisdom is the *Verbum spirans amorem*, the Word breathing forth love, the source and archetype of that sort of wisdom in man which St Thomas calls *sapida scientia*; in Gardeil's phrase, a *connaissance toute cordiale*, an understanding which springs not just from the brain but from the heart.

of the Light' (12³⁶), sons of the Sun, because the Sun had established his tabernacle within them; they were become truly a *gens regia*, a kingly race, because in giving him their faith they had opened wide their gates to give entrance to the King of Glory (*Ps.* 23⁷, ⁹), and he, by dwelling with them, had given them to share in his own kingship, so that they could speak with authority and power and direct their own ways with wisdom because they were now living in the Truth and the Truth was within them. So he was to tell Pilate, who stands as a symbol of 'worldly' kingship, of aggressive imperialism, of power-politics and political expediency: 'This is what my kingship means; I was born, I came into the world, to bear witness to the truth, and whoever has the truth in him will listen to my voice: so the truth will make him free, the truth will make him a king through sharing in my kingship'.[1]

Of necessity he will listen to the voice precisely because it is not speaking from without, an alien voice to which he can close his ears, but is the indwelling Truth speaking within him, a voice which, far from being alien, is now through that indwelling and 'interinanimation' become his own: the Truth has made it his own voice and in so doing has made him royally free, *dominus sui*, 'his own master', not a slave, but himself a king.

[1] It was in order to bring these ideas together and so perhaps make the concept of *Logos* seem less strange to the modern reader that I expanded the single line of *John* 1² into lines 4–9 of the prologue as printed here: the uncreated and creative Word is the Wisdom and Son of the Father who was with the Father from all eternity, 'before the world was made and time began'.

The Word who is infinite Light is also infinite Life. To be thus dwelling in and indwelt by the Word is therefore to be already in possession of 'that life which is eternal'. I have used this phrase generally throughout the gospel as a translation of John's *zōē aiōnios*, hoping thus to bring out two important facts: first, 'eternal' does not merely mean unending or everlasting: eternity is to be thought of not as an infinite prolongation of our earthly life-in-time but as an entirely different *kind* of life; secondly, though that other life belongs not to the earth or the cosmos but to heaven, still it must not be thought of as simply synonymous with 'otherworldly': eternity is indeed in one sense the 'life of the age to come', but in another sense it is attainable here and now, since the children of light, who have the Life dwelling within them, must in some sense live by his life. (So St Thomas Aquinas will say of the happiness of heaven that it can be enjoyed even in this world, not of course in its fullness but 'inchoatively', in its beginnings.)

Nevertheless, just as when light was made in the primal genesis of things it did not abolish the darkness, so now the children of light must still know darkness and battle with darkness for as long as they remain in what the baptismal liturgy describes as the 'night of this world'. They live in a world of *chiaroscuro*, a world of simultaneous light and darkness, life and death, joy and sorrow, good and evil; but it is a world in which these pairs of opposites do not merely co-exist but must meet in creative union in order to produce life, the light being born out of the darkness and joy fashioned out of sorrow and good established through the agony, the struggle of redeeming, transfiguring, and so integrating the evil. Consequently, the only language adequate to express the realities of our human situation will often prove to be the language of paradox, and therefore the language of symbol since the great universal symbols are of their nature ambivalent or polyvalent.

It is through symbol and paradox that the Word communicates his message and manifests himself to us. And John, who brings us the words of the Word, embraces simultaneously in his eagle-vision earth and heaven, time present and the age to come, events as history and events as revealing-symbol; he shows us the paradox-pattern of Christ's 'dark journey' and its relevance for all who, looking for the light, must follow in the footsteps of the Light, seeing by faith how their own journey is made possible because of his; and therefore the vehicle of his own communication too is the word or phrase of double or multiple meaning. It is this, coupled with his power to evoke the background of the Old Testament and, through his use of the universal symbols, the wider background of the yearnings and searchings of all humanity, which gives us as we study his language a feeling of unfathomable depth—and which makes any attempt to convey his thought in another tongue so formidably difficult.

John has no interest in historical accuracy where the time or the sequence of events is concerned: the viewpoint from which he writes will be now the time of the events he is describing and then, an instant later, the time at which he is writing; and in arranging his narrative his order is not chronological but logical and theological—he groups together incidents which form complementary or contrasting symbols in order to present a complete picture of their theological implications, as the wedding feast at Cana and the cleansing of the temple are put together in order to show us the true value of material things: that they are good, they are God's handiwork, they are to be hallowed and enjoyed, but they are to be kept in their place[1] and not allowed to usurp the place of God or hinder the worship of God or blind us to the presence of the life-giving Spirit—and John's account of the cleansing includes the symbolically significant fact that while our Lord drives out of the temple all the people who are making it a market-place, his spoken rebuke is addressed only to those who are selling doves.

What John does concern himself with and convey to us through his ambivalences is the way in which truths, events, words, may apply equally and simultaneously to different levels of existence, may for instance have both a divine and human, or an eschatological and a here-and-now application. And one of the most striking charac-teristics of his style is his use of words which have two strongly contrasting meanings—let us say baldly, his use of puns—in order to communicate the profoundest truths.

The principal examples of this include such words as light and darkness, life and death, truth, spirit, flesh, the world, and of course 'word' itself. (The title of this book,

[1] cf. *infra*, p. 60.

with its studied ambiguity—the eagle's message or the
Word as seen by the eagle—was chosen with this in
mind.) The Greek word *pneuma* can mean wind or breath
or spirit or the holy Spirit: the difficulty about translating
our Lord's words to Nicodemus in 3^8 is that they mean
simultaneously 'The wind blows where it will' and 'The
Spirit breathes where he will'; I have tried to convey
some hint of this in the text by using the noun 'breath' in
both parts of the sentence so as to link wind and Spirit
together. Again, as we have seen, against the background
of the Hebrew *Shekinah* the word 'glory' can mean either
a created manifestation of God's presence or the uncreated Word of God himself; and for this reason I have
ventured to write, in 1^{14}, 'we saw with our own eyes the
Lord's Glory': they saw the glory of the Lord Jesus, and
at the same time in so doing they saw God ('He who has
seen me has seen the Father', 14^9) in the person of the
divine Word who is God's Glory.

In the same way it would often seem correct, and
sometimes necessary, to personify such words as light and
life and truth when they are used to denote the Son of
God; but for the most part I have refrained from writing
these words with a capital letter lest the meaning should
thereby be unwarrantably narrowed down. The word
'light' for instance is used literally of the daylight and
metaphorically of spiritual enlightenment; it is also used
as a synonym for our Lord; without a capital letter this
last meaning might not be obvious in such phrases as 'to
proclaim the coming of the Light'; on the other hand
when our Lord declares that he is the light of the world

the capital would serve no useful purpose and might obscure the manifold richness of light as a symbol.

This identification of Word with Light may be seen first of all in general against the background of light and fire and sun as universal symbols of life and of the integrating or redeeming processes through which life in its fullness is sought and found.[1]

2. Faith and Transfiguration

The portrayal of those processes, alike of psychological integration and of spiritual rebirth, is first sensed in the daily journey of the sun, coming forth at dawn from the sea-dragon and 'exulting as a giant to run his course', rising at noon to the zenith, and then sinking down through the western sky to seek renewal again in the darkness of the maternal night-waters. But to find life one must have the courage not merely to go down into the darkness but to do battle there, to slay and conquer the dragon as in Babylonian myth the sun-hero Marduk conquers Tiamat the sea-dragon of the dark chaos-waters, and in Egypt Horus conquers Set, the crocodile-god of the Nile; for in this picture life is attained only when light triumphs over darkness; the darkness must be dispelled, scattered, there must be a 'harrowing of hell', though it may first have to be achieved—as in the Christ-journey it

[1] For a fuller treatment of most of the symbols referred to in these pages, and in general of the relevance to christian reality of the 'dark journey' pattern, cf. my *The Paradise Tree* and *The Water and the Fire*.

was achieved—through the sacrificial death of the hero. So, as the Word died there was darkness over the whole earth and then the darkness was shattered and scattered by the spear-point of light of resurrection; but we for our part are told that when, very early in the morning, Mary of Magdala made her way to the tomb it was still dark: the glory of the new light shines forth for all to see but it must remain hidden from men until they make their own arduous journey through their own darkness in order to find it.

The sun-hero then is a warrior, fierce as well as tender, scorching and shrivelling as well as bringing life and healing. In the story of Daphne, Phoebus Apollo the life-bringer appears as a predatory destructive agent from whom she flees—but to run away from the dangerous challenge of life is to doom oneself to the death of inertia and immobility, and she is punished for her refusal by being turned into a tree: the life-bringer will be creative for us and in us only in so far as we accept his destructive activity, the thrust of the sword or lance, the purgatorial fire which scorches and consumes in order to transmute our human dross into the gold of the divine Fire. So the mystic prays, *Hic ure, hic seca*: Here on earth may the fire burn me clean and the clean sword cut and cleave till I am refashioned in integrity; and John Donne begs God to 'breake, blowe, burn and make me new':

for I
Except you enthrall mee, never shall be free,
Nor ever chast, except you ravish mee.

In the Old Testament, fire is sometimes a manifestation of God, as when the smoke and flame wreathing about the mountain-tops announce the divine presence; sometimes it denotes God himself, as in the statement in *Deuteronomy*, which will be echoed in the *Epistle to the Hebrews*, that God is 'a consuming fire'; sometimes again it refers to the divine transfiguring process, the divine alchemy, whereby man is purified and enlightened till he becomes incandescent, sharing in the nature of fire and sun like the saints with their haloes, the children of the Light, the sons of the Sun. Daniel remains unhurt alike in the fiery furnace and the lions' den—as symbols, golden sun and golden lion are closely related—because of this affinity; he and his companions are often referred to as the three 'children' in the furnace (misinterpreting the *pueri* of the Vulgate) and this, though historically inaccurate, is symbolically most apt: as a child, endowed with the child-wisdom proper to those who have been 'born anew, from on high'[1] (as against the worldly competence of the 'false civilization' represented by the king of Babylon), Daniel remains unhurt because he is unsullied: he is a child of light and so there is no dross in him for the fire to devour, and nothing unnatural in him, nothing hostile to nature, for the wild beasts to devour. The king was amazed to see in the furnace not three men but four, and the fourth seemed as it were the son of God. If we identify this mysterious figure symbolically with the Sun of God who is also the Lion of Judah we gain further insight into the reason for Daniel's immunity:

[1] cf. *Jn.* 3³.

the child, born anew from on high, is unhurt by the fire because he is himself fire, for he lives now in the Fire and the Fire lives in him. And what is it that gives a man his solar nature, his fire-nature? St John tells us in one word: faith.

Our Lord said: 'While you still have the light with you, put your faith in the light; so you will become children of the light'. Faith is the one essential condition, on our side, of that transfiguring process whereby men are born anew from on high and begin to live in the light, the fire, the truth, begin to live with that life which is eternal. Just as there are no parables in *John* because the whole gospel is a parable, so there is no transfiguration-story in *John* because the whole gospel is a showing of the Glory and at the same time a showing of how man is transfigured through giving his faith to that Glory. Once faith is given, the Fire can begin its work—and it is the Fire, not man, who does the transfiguring. The Sun is both creative and destructive; but in either case, being the source of strength and power, is always the agent; it is always through the Word that creation and re-creation are brought about. All that man can do at this point is to make himself receptive, by faith, of the re-creative power. And so when the Jews ask our Lord, 'What are the works God would have us do?' he tells them: 'One work God asks of you: an enduring faith in him whom he has sent' ($6^{28, 29}$).

But what does this faith imply? In the story of the court official who went to Cana to beg Jesus to cure his son (4^{46} *sqq.*) it is at first sight surprising to find our Lord apparently rebuking him for his lack of faith: 'Unless you see wonders and prodigies, all of you, you refuse to believe'. Surely if the man had not believed he would not have come? But to believe in a person's power is not the same as to believe in the person; one might for instance have enough 'faith in Lourdes' to go there and pray for the gift of faith. It is only at the end of the story that St John tells us the man 'gave his faith wholly to Jesus'. Thus the condition of receiving life eternal is first of all faith as opposed to activist piety, to self-reliant good works; and secondly it is faith in the sense not of a purely intellectual assent to certain facts or statements about God but of a personal commitment to God: not simply a 'believing that' but a 'believing in' which implies self-giving and self-dedication, an acceptance not merely of the fact of the Fire but of the activity of the Fire.[1]

That activity is, as we have seen, both destructive and creative, both purgative and illuminative; it hurts in order to heal, it takes us down into darkness and death in order to bring us into light and life. In other words it causes us to follow Christ and imitate his own dark journey. The fourth gospel emphasizes the idea of looking for life in death and light in darkness by its use of the word *hypsoun*, to be lifted up, to signify simultaneously the crucifixion and the ascension of the Son of Man; the two chronologically distinct moments are here fused into one; the suffering Servant of Yahweh is at the same time 'God reigning from the wood', from the 'tree beauteous

[1] cf. *infra*, p. 41.

and splendid',[1] just as on the other hand the risen Christ will demonstrate to Thomas the reality of his wounds in hands and side.

Passion and glory are indeed successive not only chronologically but logically inasmuch as the Passion leads to the glorifying of Christ himself (his rising from the dead and his being lifted up to the right hand of the Father) and then that glory is the direct cause of the glory and wonder of Pentecost, the coming down of divine life to humanity.[2] Nevertheless it is our Lord himself who, as the darkness falls upon him and Judas goes out into the darkness, tells the others: 'Now is the Son of Man glorified' ($13^{30, 31}$). The tree *is* glory, and for two reasons. First it is the final and complete glorifying of the Father by the Son: 'Now is the Son of Man glorified, and God is glorified in him' (13^{31}). And in that giving of glory Christ himself is, so to speak, fulfilled, for he is (as John would say) the 'true Glory': it is the Sun's nature to be radiant, to be glorious but also to give glory. Secondly, the tree is glory because men find life and glory through gazing upon it: the Son of Man is to be lifted up like that serpent in the wilderness (3^{14}; *Num.* 21^9) of which the Lord God had said that whosoever gazed upon it should live: he is to be lifted up in order that those who gaze upon him, in faith, may have

[1] cf. the lines from the hymn *Vexilla Regis*: *Regnavit a ligno Deus*, and *Arbor decora et fulgida*. So also in this gospel Christ's final word on the cross is not the *lama sabachthani* of dereliction but the cry of triumphant achievement, 'The work is done'. (Not that the two are incompatible: *Ps.* 21, of which the former is the opening line, itself ends in triumph.)

[2] cp. *Jn.* 7^{39}: 'As yet the Spirit had not been given since Jesus had not yet been raised to glory.'

the life which is eternal (3^{15}) and, as St Paul tells the
Corinthians, may become transfigured into the likeness of
his glory, reflecting it as in a mirror and so borrowing
glory from that Glory (2 *Cor.* 3^{18}).

'We saw with our own eyes the Lord's Glory': in
order to have the transfiguring vision it is necessary first
of all to look for it, and to undertake the quest not for the
wrong reasons, like the Jews who had had their fill of bread
once and wanted it again (6^{26}), but like the two disciples of
the Baptist who, when Jesus asked them what they were
seeking replied in effect that they were not seeking a
'what' at all but a 'who', and begged to be told where he
was dwelling, and then went, and saw, and stayed with
him all the rest of that day: having first sought and found
the place where the Glory dwells it is then necessary,
secondly, to gaze long and deeply, obeying the injunction
of *Ps.* 45^{11} to be still and in that stillness gaze, till sight
becomes adjusted and the eyes begin truly to discern and
so to mirror the Glory. But again it is essentially at the
Glory on the Tree that we must gaze, alike for truth-
revealing vision—when they have lifted up the Son of
Man, then they will realize it was for him they were
looking (7^{28})—and for transfiguring power—and therefore the account of Christ's death ends with the quotation
from Zechariah, 'They shall look on him whom they
pierced', which in the original prophecy is immediately
preceded by the promise of abundant outpourings of
grace (*Jn.* 19^{37}; *Zech.* 12^{10}).

The piercing of Christ's side with the lance further
emphasizes the element of destruction or pain in the

re-creative process. The water and blood which flow from the wound clearly symbolize the sevenfold *mystērion* or *sacramentum*, and specifically the baptismal rebirth and the eucharistic nourishment, through which those who gaze in faith are given a share in the life and the light and the glory; but this transfiguring process is not magic: the power flows out from the tree but if it is to be effective the recipient cannot be merely passive, he must mirror the Glory in the sense of imitating in some way this piercing of the heart of God.

The lance or sword is a sun-symbol; what is said of water, that it both kills and quickens, applies to the lance as it does to the fire. It kills in order to give life, destroys in order to create; and more specifically it divides or separates in order to fashion a 'new creature'. When Adam fell from his first integrity, when he and his world disintegrated, he in that sense returned to dark chaos, though even then the hope of rebirth was given him. Now, the promise is fulfilled, the hope can be immediately realized; but the re-creation must follow the pattern of creation, the cutting and cleaving of the chaos-waters. So in the *Apocalypse* it is said of the Son of Man, who underwent death but lives eternally and is seen with face like the sun as it shines at its zenith and with eyes like flaming fire, that from his mouth there comes a two-edged sword (1[15, 16]).

This is the key to the gospel-paradox of peace and the sword. Christ declared he had come to spread fire over the earth (*Lk.* 12[49]), to bring not peace but a sword (*Mt.* 10[34]): on the other hand he told his disciples before he left them

that he was bequeathing them his peace (*Jn.* 14²⁷). But
his peace does not preclude troubles and struggles and
tensions, it supposes them: 'I give you, not the peace the
world understands and has to give, but my peace which
will not allow distress to overcome you or to make you
play the coward but will keep you always in good heart'
(*ibid.*). Similarly the purpose of the sword is not such as
the world understands—or as Simon Peter understood it,
if we view the incident symbolically, in the garden of
agony: it is to be used not to strike others (on whom
perhaps we project our own guilt, and in so doing bring
about a state of war) but to destroy in ourselves those
elements which are alien to the light, and in so doing
create in ourselves a state of peace. So the martyrs can be
peaceful and merry even in the moment of their martyrdom. And for them it is literally by the sword or its
equivalents that final integrity is achieved, the re-
creative process is completed. For most, the sword is
metaphorical, as it was for the mother of Jesus, the sorrow
of whose com-passion was her mode of living out, and so
gaining the fruits of, the Passion of her Son.

St John's story of that Passion is very rich in symbolism,
but it contains no 'signs' (as the term is used in this
gospel) since in one sense it is itself the supreme sign, the
sign of Jonah the prophet, the sign of the cross, though in
another sense it is not a sign at all and is never so called,
since it is in fact the reality—in John's terminology the
'truth'—to which the signs all point. His gospel presents
us with three different kinds of *figura*, words or events
which point to and reveal and communicate a reality

beyond themselves. There are the 'signs' (*sēmeia*), which are our Lord's miracles; there are his *paroimiai* or quasi-allegorical utterances, the 'symbol' of 10^6, the 'veiled words' of 16^{25}; and there are all the symbols in general, verbal or factual, which we find throughout the gospel.

3. Signs and Symbols

The meaning of *sēmeion* is most easily grasped by contrasting it with the 'wonders and prodigies' of which our Lord spoke to the court official at Cana. The Jews demanded—and Satan in his tempting of Christ suggested—the performance of marvels as a proof of power and an inducement to the people to give him their allegiance. 'What sign can you show us that will *make* us believe you?' the Jews asked him (6^{30}); but true faith involves understanding as well as allegiance; and as our Lord's reply to Satan was that he would not defy his Father for the sake of winning a cheap and shallow allegiance, so his reply to the Jews was in effect that he would not win their support by a parade of power such as even false prophets might provide for them (*Mt.* 24^{24}) and which would dazzle them with its glory without giving them any understanding of the Glory: he would give them only the sign of Jonah the prophet, which is to say, himself, the Son of Man, journeying for three days like Jonah in the dark waters (*Lk.* 11^{30}; *Mt.* 12^{38}; 16^{14}).

In other words, when Christ works his miracles he is not merely supporting his claims and his teaching by manifestations of power which have no intrinsic connection with those claims or that teaching; the 'signs' may induce the beholders to believe but on the other hand, as John makes clear to us, they may provoke argument and dissent; like the sword they are divisive, their effect is both life and death, belief and unbelief; they are a challenge, and it is in its choice of response to them that the world is already judged, and sentence already passed (3^{18}). For they are not mere indications that the kingdom of God is at hand; they are revelations, communications of a reality which is already there in the midst of them and which is the Light, the Life, the Truth, the Power which can and does carry out the transfiguring and integrating process, and the Glory which crowns it; and they are themselves part of that reality: the Light giving sight to the blind, the Bread giving food to the needy, the Life giving integrity to the cripple and waking Lazarus from his sleep.

They are signs therefore not so much because they point to something beyond themselves as because they point to what is implicit in themselves: to understand them—as the crowd which had been given the miraculous bread did not—is to have some understanding of what Christ himself is, and therefore the acceptance of them for what they are does not merely lead to a giving of faith but is itself a giving of faith.

It is in this sense that Christ's own journey through darkness into glory is the supreme *sēmeion*, since the lifting up of the Son of Man is the supreme revealing of God as here and now accessible, and of the divine gift of life eternal (and the divine transfiguring power which leads to it) as here and now given to those who gaze on him in faith; it is also the supreme revealing to mortal eyes of what God is like, of the immensities of his love and his pity, since it was because God 'so loved the world that he gave his only Son to be lifted up for the world's sake; that all who, gazing upon him, have faith in him may not perish but may have within them the life which is eternal' (3[16]). And finally it is the supreme revealing of God not only through Christ but in Christ, as he himself told the Jews: 'When you have lifted up the Son of Man, then you will realize that I AM' (8[28]).

These last two words (in Greek *egō eimi*) occur a number of times in *John* with a complement, as in 'I am the door'; twice where they are used absolutely the meaning is simply 'It is I'[1] but there are other examples of the absolute use where this cannot be the meaning, and where no other complement can be supplied from the context. In these cases the meaning must be sought in similar passages in the Old Testament, especially the book of Isaiah, where the words are spoken by God himself and echo his revealing of his name to Moses, in

---

[1] As the blind man uses these words in 9[9] to mean 'Yes, I am the man' so our Lord uses them to identify himself to the disciples on the lake (6[20]) and to those who come to arrest him in the garden (18[5]). But in these last two cases it is not unreasonable to discern, behind the immediate meaning, the overtones which are certainly to be found in the third group of examples discussed here, the echoes of the divine name and the divine power, and therefore in 18[5] to see a causal connection between the speaking of the words and the shrinking back of Christ's adversaries, and in 6[20] to suggest as an alternative translation, 'Do not be afraid. It is I: I AM with you'.

Exodus 3^{14}, as 'He who is' or, more literally, 'I am', the continuous present tense denoting a timeless existence without beginning or end, in other words, eternity. Here then, in the sentence from *John* just quoted (8^{28}), as also in 8^{24}, 'you shall indeed die in your sin unless you believe that I AM', and most clearly of all in 8^{58}, 'Before Abraham was born I AM', Jesus is declaring his own eternity, and thereby his divinity.

It is because of this echoing of the divine name that in these passages the 'I AM' is so written, in capitals; but I have used the capitals also in other places, where the verb is followed by a complement, especially if the complement is one of the symbolical titles with which our Lord identifies himself, since it is difficult not to see in these also an allusion to the absolute use: so, for instance, Christ is the bread, but it is the bread coming from heaven, the divine food; he is the door, but it is the door which gives entry into heaven and so joins heaven and earth, and which therefore is the divine mediator, the God-Man.

Our Lord's identification of himself with such symbols, and his working out of what is thereby implied, constitute the johannine *paroimiai*, the second of the three types of *figura* mentioned above; these supplement the *sēmeia* or signs, and are in turn supplemented by all the other symbolic words and events which occur in the course of the gospel, so that from all together we derive a rich and profound awareness both of the incarnate Word himself and of the way in which his dark journey and his lifting up bring about the re-creation and transfiguring of man.

But to understand the full richness of the gospel symbols it is important to see them, not in isolation, but
against the background, first of all of the Old Testament
writings, and then, more generally, of the universal
imagery of mankind as a whole, the language in which,
down through the ages and still today, mankind has
expressed and expresses—in myth and ritual, in poetry
and painting, in folklore and fairy-tale, in fantasy and
in the world of dreams—its deepest yearnings and
aspirations.

When the gospels tell us that something was done by
our Lord 'that the scriptures might be fulfilled', we must
not think of the action as conditioned by the necessity of
conforming to the words of a prophet or the events of
biblical history; it is the other way round: the prophetic
words were spoken in pre-vision of what would take place
in the 'hour' of fulfilment, and the historical events were
not only events but also pre-figurings, through the
medium not of language but of real life, of those greater
events, the 'true' realities,[1] which were to come. So the
sublimities and immensities of St John's prologue are
interrupted by his reference to the Baptist: it is because
in the Baptist the old order reaches its conclusion, and
when he bears witness to Christ it is the Old Testament
witnessing that 'this is the Man' of whom the biblical
prophecies and histories tell, to whom they point, and in
whom their partial revealings of God, and of man as
destined for God, are united and completed and brought
to their fulfilment.

[1] cf. pp. 46–7.

But it is not only (though it is in a special sense) the Old Testament that is fulfilled in Christ: as St Paul tells the Ephesians, the whole of history, the whole cosmic process, is fulfilled in him, 'all that is in heaven, all that is on earth, summed up in him' (1^{10}). It is not surprising therefore that the great symbols of the gospel are to be found also, not only in the Old Testament, but universally in the art and literature, the myth and religious ritual, of humanity: on the contrary, it would be surprising if they were not, for they are in fact part of humanity as such, and through them, in Kerényi's phrase, 'the world speaks'. It is sometimes felt that to link pagan myth with judaeo-christian mystery in this way is to suggest that the latter is as 'unreal' as the former; but this is a misunderstanding of the term 'myth' as it is now used in such contexts: it means simply 'a sacred iconograph', that is, an image which communicates sacred or religious reality; it says nothing as to whether the image is derived from human history or human fantasy—and in fact the source of the image makes no difference to the validity of the communication: the value to us of the book of Tobias or of our Lord's story of the prodigal son remains exactly the same whether the people concerned were 'real' people or not.

But substantially the story of mankind as told in the Bible is indeed history, precisely because its purpose is to show us how the unfolding of the story leads up to—and prophetically and symbolically adumbrates—its fulfilment in Christ, and how that fulfilment is the fulfilment of a definite divine promise. Thus we have to make a triple distinction: the pagan myths and rituals express man's deepest yearnings, his yearning for immortal life and youth; the Old Testament expresses not merely a yearning but a hope, and a hope firmly based upon a divine promise; the New Testament shows us the fulfilment of the promise and the hope (and *a fortiori* of the yearnings) in the person of the incarnate Word, who lived out the myth-pattern in actual historical fact in his own life and death and rising again from the dead in order that we might thereby be empowered to live it out in our own different ways ourselves. And as the power to do this comes to us mainly through the christian *mystērion*, the sevenfold *sacramentum*, and especially through the water of baptism and the bread of the Mass, so we find there also, in the significant and effective sacramental ritual, the same pattern expressed in the same symbols.

There is this further difference between the biblical and non-biblical presentations of the pattern: the Old Testament pre-figurings, though incomplete and fragmentary, are true indications so far as they go; the Bible is, after all, God's own book; in pagan mythology and ritual, on the other hand, as generally in poems written and tales told by men, we shall expect to find distortions of the pattern, not merely a partial but a faulty vision; but we should not on that account despise them or fight shy of them: given a sure grasp of the truth of the christian *mystērion*, we can derive immense help and enlightenment from the purely human expressions of the biblical themes: they can pour new life for us into images which over-familiarity has dulled, they can bring to light implications which we had not noticed, with each new insight they can take us a little deeper into the unsoundable depths of the theological content of the pattern, and at the same time they can show us precisely the universality of the truths and facts of which the scriptures and the christian *mystērion* speak to us, and the naturalness and humanness of the christian ideal of holiness; they can help us to find courage to accept the truth of christianity and its challenge inasmuch as they can make us see—since they are the cry of humanity as such, the whole world speaking in and through them—that the truth and the challenge are in fact the fulfilment of the deepest longings of the human heart.

4. *Light and Darkness*

> *Mors et vita duello*
> *conflixere mirando:*
> *dux vitae mortuus*
> *regnat vivus:*

so the Easter hymn, the *Victimae paschali*, describes how death and life are locked together in a strange and wonderful combat, at the end of which 'the champion of life lies dead and yet victoriously lives and reigns'. St John's prologue takes us to the heart of this drama (and the fourth gospel is indeed cast in dramatic form): the Light came down into the world and shone out in the darkness of the world; but the world would not welcome it, nor could the darkness master it. At the same time we are straightway confronted with the ambivalence which lies at the heart of this antithesis between light and darkness, death and life. By 'the world' we are sometimes to understand the earth and its inhabitants, or more particularly the world of humanity (and sometimes indeed it means simply 'everybody', *tout le monde*), but sometimes 'this world' is contrasted with the heavenly world, it is the kingdom of Satan as opposed to the kingdom of God, and comprises those who repudiate the light and prefer the darkness.

Darkness therefore is also, in that context, an ethical concept: as light and glory manifest the divine presence and it is in 'light inaccessible' that God dwells, so darkness is both the sign and the dwelling-place of the mystery of iniquity, of 'him who has lorded it over this world', and of those who obey him and so make themselves a part of 'the Evil which is in the world'. On the other hand, as death is that from which life springs, and the tomb is the womb, so also night begets light, it is out of darkness that light is engendered—an Orphic poem speaks of night as *pantōn genesis*, the birth of all things— as in the beginning it was from the dark chaos-waters that the earth was fashioned and light and life were made; the journey to life and integrity lies through darkness, since it is an arduous search, a quest involving danger and struggle and terror and loneliness (though the greyness of the Vergilian underworld-journey—

ibant obscuri sola sub nocte per umbram,

'darkly they journeyed through the shadows, with night as their only shelter'—cannot exactly characterize the journey of the christian who, as *comes Solis*, the companion of the Sun, is never, even in his darkest moments, wholly bereft of the Sun's sustaining power).

In the gospel then, while night and darkness are mentioned as physical facts, circumstances of historical events, as also is noon, the zenith of the sun's splendour, they can also signify moral evil, hatred and rejection of the Light, a rejection springing from a proud and culpable blindness of heart which, if it grows so deep-rooted as to be immovable, becomes the ultimate darkness of hell; on the other hand they can signify the darkness which is the womb of light; and in the dramatic moment when Judas goes out from the supper-room to the betrayal all these significations come together: Judas goes out into the 'exterior darkness' of an irrevocable choice of evil which will be followed only by the deathly sterility of remorse; Peter too goes down into the darkness of moral evil, his own betrayal (by denial) of Jesus, but he finds in the darkness the waters of creative sorrow, and so the cock-crow heralds the dawn of his new and greater day;[1] above all it is on and for the Word himself that the night falls to summon him to that furthermost descent into the world's darkness which is also his final and supreme 'lifting up'.

The New Testament fulfils the Old not by continuing it but by replacing it with a new order of things: 'a new life for us in place of the old: no longer simply the law as given to man by Moses, but life, gracious and true,

[1] In primitive times the christian liturgy, celebrated at night, ended at cock-crow.

brought to man by Christ' (cp. 1[17-18]): the water is changed into wine; the man-made temple is replaced by the theandric[1] *templum non manufactum*; the ritual cleansings of the Baptist, who baptizes 'only with water', give way to the baptism 'of water and the Spirit' which brings about in real life what the ritual expresses in symbol. And as the world is thus given a new genesis[2] and is born again as a new creation through the agency of the second Adam, so every man who would belong to this new order must himself be born 'anew from on high' through faith in the new Adam. But faith is not just an intellectual judgement, it is a personal commitment: to give your faith to Christ is to give yourself to Christ, to put your faith in Christ is to put yourself and your fate in his hands; and this in turn means welcoming and accepting the Light, and being possessed of—and still more possessed by—the Truth. Through the creative Word the light of understanding is given to every man who comes into the world (1[9]), but the light of faith is given, through the saving and re-creative Word, only to those who welcome the Light and its power to transfigure them

[1] i.e. divine and human.

[2] So the opening words of the fourth gospel are the same as those of *Genesis*: In the beginning . . .; and it is tempting to see a multiple echo, and perhaps a hint of personification, implied in the difficult text of 8[25] where our Lord answers the direct question, Who are you? with *tēn archēn hoti kai lalō hymin*: I AM what I told you from the beginning; I AM from the beginning, as I told you; As I told you, I am He Who Is from the beginning—which last reading is not so remote from the suggestive (though textually dubious) Vulgate rendering, *principium qui et loquor vobis*, 'I, who am now speaking to you, I AM the source from whom all life, all genesis, springs'.

into the likeness of the Light so that they come to live in the Light.

The commitment of faith is thus a total commitment. The Light, the Truth, is infinite and all-embracing not only in the sense of comprising in himself all that is true but also in the sense of engaging the whole personality of the believer. It is possible for the mind to accept some partial truth or light while the personality as a whole remains in darkness; but one cannot give oneself wholly in faith to the Light and yet remain in darkness.

As we have seen, the eternal *Logos* is first of all the self-knowledge of God and the utterance of that knowledge within the Godhead; secondly, the *Logos* is expressed in those external utterances which are God's revealing of himself to his creatures, a revealing through 'words' but in the Hebrew sense of 'words' as comprising both words and deeds or events; and this revealing culminates in the coming of the Word himself into the world as man, and in the words he then spoke, the works he performed, the events which made up his life amongst us. But the message thus brought to us comprises not only *rhēmata* or sayings but *entolai* or commands, for the revealing of God includes the revealing of his will, his purpose or, in St Paul's phrase, his 'loving design'; it includes therefore that 'law' which Christ came not to destroy but to transfigure and so bring to its fulfilment: we are still, we are much more than before, to sing the praises of the law as does the psalmist, but remembering always that the content of the law is not simply 'precepts' but (as the Vulgate of *Ps.* 118 has it) *testimonia*: the law is light and enlightenment; it is God's revealing of his designs for and his ways with man, and of man's way to God: and it is precisely because the 'new life' which we have been given is 'no longer simply the law as given to man by Moses but life, gracious and true, brought to man by Christ' (1^{17}) that at all costs we have to avoid the legalism which our Lord so constantly attacked and so strongly condemned, and which in fact destroys the law—'the letter kills'—by taking it out of its setting of design and purpose and separating it from its *ratio*, its 'reasoned' basis—which is to say, in the last resort, from the *Logos*.

We have our Law, our *Torah*, and it is God's command for us; but we have at all costs to make sure that we see it as it really is, our *Tao*, the way to Life, and a way which is itself Life. *Omnes viae tuae veritas*, *Ps.* 118 tells us: all God's ways are truth; his ways with us and his designs for us are law for us, but they are also the revealing of truth to us, and therefore the source of life for us: 'your law is truth', the same psalm declares—not just 'is true' but 'is the truth', and the truth 'makes us free' since it brings us out of the domain and the domination of darkness and into the realm of light, and to live in the light, to be a son of the Sun, is in turn to live in and by the new life, the true life, God's life, since it is to have the true *gnōsis*, the God-given wisdom which is an understanding of God: for 'this is life eternal: to know, lovingly, and to glorify you, the only true God, and him whom you sent—God's messenger, man's Messiah—Jesus' (cp. *Jn.* 17^3).

Thus when our Lord says that the Truth will make us free we are not to take this as meaning that the Messiah

43

will make us free and that he happens also to be referred
to sometimes as the truth: it is the truth as such that
makes free men of us by giving us 'life full and abounding': the whole purpose of our dark journey, the object
of our quest in this temporal life, is to arrive at the knowledge of the divine and life-giving and transfiguring
truth which is the full revealing to us of God and of his
purpose in the person of the incarnate Word.

And it is precisely because the Truth is himself a person, not just a proposition, that faith is a personal
commitment and not just an intellectual assent to proposi-
tions, and that the life which is eternal is the loving knowledge of God and his Christ. But to arrive at the knowledge
of the truth means to discover the truth: a quest is, by
definition, a voyage of discovery. We are all looking,
searching, groping for something (and the idea of this
universal quest is evoked by the 'What are you looking
for?' of the gospel),[1] and often we do not know what we
are looking for except that it is something which will
give meaning to our lives—and so we have to learn first
that 'meaning' is *logos* and in the last resort is the *Logos*;
and therefore with Simon Peter we have to ask ourselves

[1] Our Lord's question and that of the two disciples (1[38]) mean,
quite simply, 'What is it? What do you want?' and 'Where are
you staying?'; but the overtones are obvious: the literal sense of
our Lord's words, 'What are you seeking?', evokes the whole idea
and imagery of the 'quest', the journey in search of reality; that of
the disciples' question, 'Where do you dwell?' evokes the idea of the
'place of God's presence', the *Shekinah*, the 'place where thy Glory
dwelleth', and the abiding of God with man, brought about
through the Word whose name is Emmanuel, 'God with us'.
Cf. *supra*, p. 28 and *infra*, p. 52.

to whom else we should go, since only the Word has the words which give life (and give meaning to life), only the Word has the secret of the life which is eternal (cp. 6^{69}): it is he who is the object of the quest, and the one essential question for us as for the two disciples of the Baptist is, 'Master, where is your dwelling-place?' (1^{38}).

To say that every man must discover the truth for himself is not to deny that faith is a gift from God or that we need to be taught by God through his revealing Word and through the Church which communicates the Word to us; it is to say that we cannot arrive at true knowledge simply by parrot-memorizings of tags of doctrine, by a shallow and facile familiarity with the necessary but necessarily inadequate formulas which express for us something of the inexpressible Reality: we do not know God in these, we are led to him through them, just as faith is not belief in a creed but belief, through a creed, in the reality about which the creed speaks to us. Every man born into the world has to look for a teacher who will show him how to use that 'light of understanding' which is his by nature; he needs to be taught the truth, but he will never possess it, still less be possessed by it, until, like one returning home and recognizing the familiar landmarks and features which are part of himself, he discovers in his heart the conviction that what he has been told is true.

We know the excitement of discovering at last the solution to a problem which has long been perplexing and fascinating us; we know in particular the excitement of gaining some new insight into a loved personality. For those who believe, the gaining of each new insight into the Truth carries with it both these joys. The labours of a Thomas Aquinas are inspired both by the passion for truth which characterizes all great thinkers and by the impassioned love of God which characterizes all the saints, but for him these are not two loves but one: in one version of his hymn, *Adoro te*, God is invoked not as 'hidden Godhead' but as *latens veritas*, 'hidden Truth', and for him heaven consists essentially in seeing God, knowing God in the immediacy of face to face vision, a vision which is perfect joy and peace because it is the final solution to all problems and perplexities and searchings as well as the final fulfilment of all desires. And this exactly accords with St John's definition of life eternal as the loving knowledge of God and of his messenger, a knowledge attained when the darkness of night finally gives way to the light which has sprung from it and has grown to the full brightness and splendour of its zenith, and when blindness is replaced by sight and reaches the completion of perfect vision, and the transfiguration of man by the light is completed and he can face the Light and gaze at the Light because he is himself light, he can gaze at the Sun like the Eagle because he is himself fire.

The Word is the 'true Light' (1⁹). John makes use of two words both meaning 'true': *alēthēs* means 'true' as opposed to 'false' or 'not according to the facts' and is applied therefore to statements or to those who make them; *alēthinos* on the other hand usually means 'real, authentic' as opposed to what is merely a partial and perhaps figurative presentation of the genuine reality. Thus the Baptist was 'a burning and shining light' but he was not the true light. Moreover, the opposite of 'true' in this sense is often 'literal': thus our Lord is the true temple, as opposed to the temple of stone, just as he is the true light for the world as opposed to the light of day in the literal sense. And it is because he thus fulfils and therefore replaces the Old Testament pre-figurings that the evangelists so often remind us how in what he does and is the scriptures are fulfilled.

But the incarnate Word is not merely the reality corresponding to the old pre-figurings: he makes effective what the pre-figurings merely signified. (So, for instance, his baptism differs from that of John, who baptized 'only with water'.) And this fact is conveyed to us by the use of the word 'living': the Jews spoke often of the 'living God', meaning by this to emphasize God's activity in the world, creating, sustaining, moving, directing, and his constant intervention in the shaping of human history. So the Word is the living bread and the living water, coming down from heaven and bringing from heaven the true life, the life which is eternal. In other words, the Truth is both the object of man's quest and the power given him to undertake the quest: Christ is the Truth, to know whom is to have life eternal, but he is also the Way to that knowledge.

In the very beginning, the first genesis of all things, God made the firmament, the solid vault of heaven, to divide the waters above from the waters below. This imagery of creating by cutting and cleaving contains the first hint of the symbolism of the sword or lance, the sword which Christ said he had come to bring, the lance with which he himself was 'divided' that the water and blood of super-vitality might flow from his side to quicken the world; and now in the Mass it is through a symbolic separation of Body and Blood—the separate consecrations of bread and wine—that the sacrificial death is represented for us; and the symbolic re-uniting which follows, in the 'commingling', and which is the representing of Christ's rising from the dead into the glory of the new life, is at once the exemplar and the cause of our own adoption into that life, an adoption which will not be fully achieved in us without the creative thrust of the sword.

But the solid vault too must be pierced, to allow of the meeting of the waters, the marriage of heaven and earth, without which—without the rain and the snow[1] to bedew the earth—there can be no green and growing things, no seed nor fruit of the earth: there must be a 'door', an aperture, to allow the worship and aspiration of man to ascend to heaven and the life and power of heaven to come down upon the earth. So it is that primitive peoples have a great tree, or put up a high pole or pillar, in the centre of their sacred places; and so in the Old Testament, when the flood came, destroying in order to renew, the fountains of the great deep broke through and the flood-gates of heaven were opened and thus the two waters,

[1] 'As the rain and the snow come down from heaven, and . . . soak the earth and water it and make it to spring, and give seed to the sower and bread to the eater, so shall my word be' (*Isaiah* 55[10–11]).

from above and below, were joined; and when Jacob had
dreamed of the ladder reaching up into heaven, and the
angels ascending and descending upon it and at the top of
it the Lord God himself leaning down, he cried out as he
awoke: 'This is a place of awe: this is the house of God:
this is the gateway into heaven.'[1]

We have an insight into the truth of all this—into its
full meaning—now that the Truth has been shown to us:
we know now that it is God himself who is our way to
God, that the aperture in the vault of heaven, the gateway
into heaven, is the Word who himself told us, 'I AM the
door', 'I AM the way', and who by implication identified
himself with the reality which Jacob's ladder pre-figured:
'You shall all see the heavens opened and the angels of
God going up and coming down upon the Son of Man',[2]
and this in turn is echoed by the words of Stephen the
first christian martyr when, gazing up at heaven and
seeing God's Glory, he cried, 'I see the heavens opened,
and the Son of Man standing at the right hand of God'.[3]

---

[1] cf. *Gen.* 28[12-18].　[2] *Jn.* 7[9]; 10[6]; 1[51].　[3] *Acts*, 7[55].

5. Christ the Way

It is, then, in the idea of the transfiguring journey, the descent and ascent, through darkness into light, through death into life, that all these great Christ-symbols coalesce. The Word, through his gift to us of the life-bringing Wind, the breath of the Spirit, makes possible and initiates the journey; the Truth, the Wisdom, gives us an understanding of it, its meaning and purpose, its challenges and perils; the Light illumines our darkness, gives sight to our eyes and is as a 'lamp for our feet';[1] the true Bread gives us the necessary strength and power, as the literal and prefigurative bread strengthened Elijah for his forty days' journey to the mount of God; the Wine enables us to meet with joy and courage the hardships and sorrows of the journey, and, as the 'fruit of the Vine', gives us that peace which will not let distress overcome us or make us play the coward but will keep us always in good heart[2] since it keeps us in Christ's heart.

Thus the Word does not merely provide us with light and enlightenment, with bread and wine, as we go on our way: he himself is the Light, the Bread, the Wine. And similarly he does not merely indicate the way to us: he himself is the Way: 'No one can go to the Father except by way of me' (14[6]); 'I AM the door of the sheepfold . . . He who enters in through me will be safe and sound; he can come and go as he will, freely' (10[7, 9]). For as the goal of the dark journey, heaven, consists essentially in knowing God, and him whom he sent, in the immediacy

[1] *Ps.* 118[105].   [2] cf. *Jn.* 15[3, 5]; 14[27].

of vision, and consequently in having the *gaudium de veritate*[1] of Augustine's definition, the 'joy of seeing the Truth', so also the dark journey itself consists essentially in a growing knowledge of God in the obscurity of faith, with its concomitant 'joy in believing'. 'I know that my Redeemer is living and true' and that therefore 'in my flesh I shall see God'[2]: the glory of the flesh of the risen Christ is the guarantee of a similar glory and integrity for those who firmly and fully give him their faith and so are transfigured into his likeness and even here on earth begin to live in and by his own life.

But to be one with Christ *in via* means to journey through darkness in other senses besides that of the obscurity of faith. The Door opens on to life, but to life through death. *Fons quasi sepultura est*, says St Ambrose:[3] the baptismal waters are the 'fountains springing up into the life which is eternal', but 'the font is tomb' as well as womb; by baptism, St Paul tells us, we are buried with Christ in his death so as to be raised up like him and with him into a new mode of existence.[4] For some, as for the blessed Stephen, it is literally through the acceptance of physical death for and with and in Christ—a giving up of one's life, whether in martyrdom or in some other mode of self-sacrifice, which is the final act of faith and love— that the heavens open and the Glory is seen; for most, it is the transfiguring effect of the various metaphorical forms of death or darkness they encounter on their way that brings the journey to its conclusion. But for all those

---

[1] *Confess.* x. 23.   [2] cf. *Job*, 19$^{25-6}$ (*Vulgate*).
[3] cf. *De Sacramentis*, II. vi. 19.   [4] cf. *Romans*, 6^4.

who have truly given their faith to Christ, if the way lies
through darkness because of its pains and sorrows, it is
also a journeying in light, and there is joy in believing,
because they look forward, humbly and in fear yet eagerly
and with the confidence of hope, to the fulfilment of the
promise, the dawning of the eternal day; and also because,
even here and now, they know that they walk in the presence and companionship of the Light even though its
glory is never fully visible and often seems to be completely
hidden from their eyes.

Like the two disciples of the Baptist, and like the neophyte as he approaches the font of baptism, they have
been asked what they are searching for and, having
answered, have been told, 'Come and see'. But going to
see God's dwelling-place involves leaving one's own: as in
every human life there comes a moment when the child
must literally or metaphorically leave his parents' home
and begin to make his own way as an adult in the world,
must cut himself off (as with a sword) from the shelter
and security of his small, familiar world to adventure in
the other, greater world, so also the christian journey
involves, not just once but frequently, a cutting away, a
separation, the destructive and creative sword. When
Jacob set out on his quest for integrity, leaving behind
him home and security and protective mother, he came
to a place called Luz; and if we derive this name from the
verb *luz*, 'to go away, turn aside', it gives us the idea of
separation. It was here that Jacob dreamed of the ladder
and was given the promise of future glory and the present
sight, in his dream, of the Lord, so that he changed the

name of the place from Luz to Bethel, the House of God.
We may compare this with the incident in the childhood
of the 'true' Jacob when, returning from a pilgrimage to
Jerusalem, his parents lost him and after a long and
anguished search found him[1] in the temple, the house of
God, and he then explained to them that this separation
must be, the moment would come when he must leave
them, in order to do the work his Father had given him
to do. (And later his disciples in their turn will be
required to 'leave all and follow' him.[2])

We find this sacrificial homelessness of the Son of Man
at the very beginning of his earthly life, his birth in the
stable-cave.

The tradition according to which Christ was born in a
cave (Lat. *spelaeum*, Gk. *spēlaion*) is of great symbolic
significance. The mythic dark journey often involves a
descent into an underground or under-sea cave; and the
cave itself may be very great, like Coleridge's 'caverns
measureless to man', but the opening which leads into it

[1] In the language of symbol, losing-and-finding is a variant of the
death-and-rebirth theme.

[2] Jesus told Nathanael that he had seen him, before Philip called
to him, 'under the fig-tree': this expression could mean simply
'over there, out of sight', or, as Lagrange suggests, there might be
an association between the fig-tree and some inner crisis in
Nathanael's life, known only to him, which would therefore reveal
to him Christ's supernatural knowledge of him; from our point of
view, however, it is important to remember that in the Old
Testament the phrase is used as an image of the peace and security
of home (e.g. III *Kings*, 4[25]: 'And Judah and Israel dwelt secure
from alarm, each man under his vine and his fig-tree'): the call of
Philip is in fact the call of Christ, bidding him leave the comfort
and security of home, and follow him.

is very small, so that one must bend down low in order to pass through it; for the cave is the womb of the new life, and as the way to wisdom is, in the words of Augustine, 'first, humility, and secondly humility, and thirdly humility', so the way to attain the new life is humble receptivity, a *kenōsis*, an emptying of the self of all egocentricity and arrogant self-reliance, without which the transfiguring work of the living and life-bringing Word cannot be carried out.[1] In the pagan mysteries also we find the *spelaeum* as the place of initiation for the neophyte—the mysteries themselves being *in-itia*, a ritual (and nocturnal) entry into the darkness where the new genesis will take place.

Among the Jews it was customary to adapt caves for use as burial-places; John explicitly says that the tomb of Lazarus was a *spēlaion*, and it is reasonable to suppose that the term would apply also to the tomb of our Lord, which the synoptics describe as hewn or fashioned out of the rock; moreover the symbolism of the small, low entry into the cave seems to be preserved in the description of the beloved disciple and Mary Magdalen bending down in order to look into it. Thus once again the two ideas of tomb and womb are united; and this union becomes the more striking if we allow the stone with which the tombs were sealed to remind us of that other 'great

[1] St Bernard, in a Christmas Eve sermon, speaks of the gospel announcement of Christ's birth as *Verbum breve de Verbo abbreviato*, 'a little word about the Word made little': to enter through the small opening of the cave one must make oneself small; this lesson is taught us by the *kenōsis* of the infant-Word in the cave.

stone' which closed the mouth of the well where Jacob
met Rachel and which, though normally it took several
men 'to roll it away', Jacob removed by himself in his
new-found strength when he saw Rachel coming towards
him (cf. *Gen.* 23$^{1-10}$); for a well is one of the forms of the
symbol of rebirth through water, and this particular well
reminds us of the story of the Samaritan woman (*Jn.* 4^{5}
sqq.) and of how Jesus 'sat down by the well for he was
weary after his journey' and in his weariness spoke of the
living water which gives renewal of life and of strength.[1]
Finally, as the pagan *mystēs* went down into his dark
spelaeum in search of life, so the early christians in time
of persecution went down into their catacombs to receive
the Life and the Light, and so at all times the christian
neophyte must go down into the baptismal waters, the
font which is tomb and womb, to be born anew from on
high into the new mode of existence, the life which is
eternal.

The homelessness of the Word, born in a stable-cave
and then in his public life having nowhere to 'lay his
head', no place he could call his own—for 'his own
received him not'—is further evoked for us by the name
with which the Baptist refers to him, the Lamb of God.
The principal allusions here are no doubt to the paschal
lamb of *Exodus* 7, and to Isaiah's description of the Man
of Sorrows as the lamb that stands silent before the
shearers (57^{7}); and the Baptist would probably have in
mind also the lamb sacrificed daily as a burnt-offering;
but it certainly seems reasonable to add to these a further

[1] cf. *infra*, pp. 61–3.

55

allusion, to the lamb of *Leviticus* 14, offered as a victim for wrong done, and from this we are inevitably led on, by the Baptist's reference to the taking away of the world's sin, to *Leviticus* 16, to the scape-goat driven out, the guilt of all Israel's sins on its head, into the 'uninhabited land' of the desert, the land that is waste and void, that the people might thereby be freed from their sins.

The meekness of the lamb, silent before the shearers, will be emphasized later on in the gospel, first in the similar imagery of the 'little donkey', the 'ass's foal', in the Palm Sunday story (riding an animal is in general a symbol of self-mastery; the modest and diminutive donkey, in contrast to the proud nobility of the horse, suggests a mastery which is not a despotism achieved through violence and arrogant self-reliance but a harmony achieved through a humble and loving domestication of the passions), and then in the reference to the silence of our Lord—*Jesus autem tacebat*—in the account of his trial.[1] On the other hand the entry into Jerusalem is a triumph, and a kingly triumph; and in the story of the Passion, John constantly stresses the way in which a power and authority not of this world emanate from our Lord so that those who come to arrest him shrink back in terror and Pilate is filled with superstitious dread, and the fact that Christ is throughout in regal command of the unfolding of events: he carries his own cross (there is no mention of Simon of Cyrene) and in the moment of death it is he who actively gives up his life (for 'no one can take it' from him).

[1] cf. *infra*, p. 105.

In the same way the Baptist's description of the Messiah combines the meekness of the Old Testament references with the majesty of the Lamb of the Apocalypse; for this is 'the man of whom I said that one would come after me who would yet take rank before me: for before I began to be, already he lived': this is 'the Son of God' ($1^{30, 34}$). Linguistic associations strengthen this 'coincidence of opposites' for us: as the Latin *ignis*, fire, is close to the Sanskrit *agnis*, personified as Agni the Sun-god, so Agni in turn suggests the Agnus Dei: the Sun, the golden Lion, *is* the Lamb, an identification which adds point to Isaiah's statement in his description of the future kingdom of God that lion and lamb shall dwell together, with a little child to lead them (11^6).

The Fire is both fierce and tender, consuming yet quickening; the Way is both rough and refreshing, a trackless and waterless desert yet also a place of pasture. At the beginning of the gospel John tells us of the tragedy of rejection: the world would not welcome the Word, the darkness would not receive the Light, the Son's own people turned him away; but he tells us also of the triumphant fruits of acceptance, of the new life replacing the old, and of how 'we saw with our own eyes the Lord's Glory . . . gracious and true'. The journey is in *chiaroscuro*; but for the children of light there should be more stress on light than on darkness, more on joy than on sorrow, precisely because for them, since the Light lives in them, darkness and sorrow are always the prelude to, and the raw material and the promise of, an ever-increasing light and deepening joy. It is not surprising therefore to find that, just as the Roman ritual of the Mass begins with a reference, emphasized by repetition, to God as the giver of youth and of joy (*Ps.* 42^4), so the first of the messianic 'signs' recorded by John is the joyous miracle of the water turned into wine at the wedding feast, and the joy here too is emphasized, and given a note of exuberance, by the filling of the water-jars 'brimful'—an adjective which will recur later when our Lord speaks of the pouring of his own joy into the hearts of his followers.

Thus this first sign, the first of our Lord's public 'works' and therefore in a sense the initiation and promulgation of the new order of things, marks that new order from the very beginning with the characteristic note of joy. It is essentially the joy of fulfilment, the fulfilling of the longings, the realizing of the hopes, of Israel through the ages. The Jewish ritual cleansings for which these water-jars had been provided remind us of our Lord's distinction between inward and outward defilement and his stern denunciation of the pharisees for their exclusive concern with the latter and in general for turning the law into a burden too heavy to be borne (cf. *Matt.* 15$^{11-20}$; 23^4): all this 'bondage of the law', the emptiness of the merely ritual cleansings[1] and the gloom of the *onera importabilia*, the unbearable burdens, are now replaced by the *gaudium de veritate*, the christian joy in

[1] cp. *Jeremiah*, 2^{13}: 'They have forsaken me, the fountain of living water, and have digged to themselves cisterns, broken cisterns, that can hold no water.'

the Truth and in the freedom the Truth bestows. The contrast between the old order and the new is emphasized by the fact that the jars were six in number, one short of the symbol of completeness; and this in turn gives colour to the suggestion (based on the fact that the verb here used for 'to draw' is properly used of drawing water from a well) that first the jars were filled with water and then the wine came from the well itself—and Christ is the 'well of living water'[1]—at the seventh drawing.

The merely ritual cleansings, the baptizings 'only with water' are replaced by the efficacy of the christian *mystērion*; and this efficacy is the fruit of the messianic work which is here initiated but which consists essentially in the 'lifting up' of the Son of Man. In giving the comment of the master of the feast—that usually not the best but an inferior wine is served when 'men have drunk deep'—I have added 'and are merry': my excuse for this is that it is sufficiently implied in the context, for guests who had not reached at least that stage of intoxication could hardly fail to notice the difference; but my reason for doing it is that the words thus echo a line from the *Book of Ruth*, 'When Boaz had eaten and drunk and was merry, he went to sleep' (3[7]), a line which Albertus Magnus in his *De Eucharistia* applies to our Lord going joyously after the supper to his 'sleep' on the cross, and this evocation is especially apt, not only because our Lord himself spoke of death as sleep,[2] but in particular because

[1] cf. preceding footnote.
[2] cf. *infra*, p. 80.

in the description of his death given by John the meaning seems to be precisely that he 'let his head sink down as though to sleep' and so 'yielded up his spirit' (19^{30}): the work of the six days of the new creation was completed, and now, for him, the seventh day, the eternal sabbath, was to begin: he could rest now from all his labours, *ab universo opere quod patrarat*.[1]

6. *The New Temple and its Worship*

In the Mass, after the initial note of joy we go on to confess our sinfulness, our refusal or betrayal of the Light and our consequent inner defilement; similarly John passes from the joy of Cana to the anger of Christ at the defiling of the temple. As we have seen, the two incidents are complementary: Cana asserts the humanness of holiness and the goodness of wine and weddings and, by implication, of material things in general; on the other hand the temple story warns us not to exaggerate their value, not to be materialists, not to allow our interest in them to make us forgetful of things of far greater value but to keep it always within the framework of God's will, his 'loving design' for us, and of our worship of him. But there is a further lesson: here too the new order of things is announced, in the substitution of the new temple, the true temple, for the old, though Christ's words are, at the time, too cryptic for his hearers. He will take up this

[1] *Gen.* 2^2.

theme again at Jacob's well: the new temple, not made with hands, requires a new kind of worship: we are not to be materialists in our worship any more than in our value-judgements; again and again in the Old Testament God had condemned the folly, and the insult, of relying simply on external rites, regardless of what is in the heart; we have to learn, not indeed to abandon ritual since he himself institutes the *mystērion* for us, but to carry out the ritual 'in spirit and in truth', making it truly the vehicle of our self-dedication to the will of the Father while at the same time, because of our giving of our faith to the Son, it becomes a 'worship which is real and life-giving' since our *sursum corda*, the lifting up of our hearts, is incorporated into the supreme act of human worship and obedience, the lifting up of the Son.

'You judge simply by appearances, by the flesh your fleshly eyes can see' (cf. 8[15]): it is the materialism of the Jews, and the legalism to which it gives rise, that blind them to the truth and make them reject the light. They ask to be shown wonders and prodigies but cannot understand the signs which are shown them; the Samaritan woman thinks the living water is merely fresh water; Nicodemus has to be made to see that water of itself is barren, it cannot be living and life-giving until, like the water of chaos, it is impregnated by the creative Wind from on high; there has to be a new birth, but it cannot be achieved by man himself, by external rituals or external rectitude. The five thousand first of all cannot grasp that the miraculous provision of food for them is unimportant compared with what it signifies; then they assume that the 'unperishing bread' can be won by activism, by a multiplication of external 'works'; and finally, still thinking according to the flesh, they are outraged by what they take to be the crude anthropophagy of the doctrine of the Bread of Life.

The living and life-giving water and the new temple and its 'real and life-giving' worship are the main themes of the story of the Samaritan woman. It is noon, the high moment of the Sun's manifestation, when Jesus comes to the well; and he sits down by it for he is weary after his journey—perhaps, as Lagrange suggests, even more weary than his disciples who have gone into the city to buy food. And in his weariness he speaks of the living water which gives renewal of life and of strength: as Augustine put it, *tibi fatigatus est*,[1] he suffered weariness for our sakes, not to save us from weariness but to enable us to suffer our weariness, like him, without losing heart, putting new life and vigour into our dulled and slothful spirits.

As so often in this gospel, initial misunderstanding is used to clarify doctrine. 'Living water' means, literally, fresh water, flowing from a spring; and when Jesus tells the woman that had she asked he would have given her 'the gift of living water' she takes the words in this sense: the water in the well comes from a spring, but the well is very deep and the surface of the water lies far below ground level: how can our Lord, without rope and bucket, draw water for her? Jesus then explains that this

[1] *Tractat. in Joann.* 15.

gift, this water, is a 'living spring' within a man, 'bearing him into the life which is eternal' (4^{14}).

In the Old Testament, 'living water' is used as a metaphor for the divine life-giving activity;[1] and 'the gift of God' refers to the revelation of truth, to the *Torah*; but there are further meanings to add to these: water is identified with the Spirit, it is in the instructing of men's hearts by the Spirit that revelation culminates, and those who are baptized into the Spirit have within them the life which is eternal; finally, one of the names given to the Spirit is the Gift—and it was with this in mind that in the text I first put the word alone before repeating it in the whole phrase, 'I would have given you the gift, the gift of living water', and indeed was tempted to print it, like the 'Glory' of 1^{14}, with a capital.

Our Lord then goes on to speak of the new temple and the worship proper to it: he is himself the temple, being the place of God's presence, but he is also the worship, being himself both priest and victim in the offering of the new sacrifice. The true worshippers of God, therefore, must henceforth offer him the worship which is 'real and life-giving': real in the sense of 'true' as John uses the word, the reality which supersedes, because it fulfils, all its pre-figurings in the Old Dispensation; and wholly real because in the christian sacrifice humanity takes part in a divine reality, the offering to God of the divine victim by the divine priest: man as God's creature is truly himself when offering himself, his life, to his Creator; he is supremely, superabundantly, himself when,

[1] cf. *supra*, p. 47.

being made one with Christ in the Spirit, his self-offering is incorporated into that of Christ; and because of that incorporation his offering becomes not only a gift to God but the supreme, and supremely life-giving, gift from God.

In his second sign, the sign of the nobleman's son, Jesus had stressed the difference between true faith in him and a mere readiness to believe in his power. Now in the third, the sign of the cripple, we are taken a step further: the new life is brought about through the meeting of the power of God from on high with the *fiat*, the humble receptivity, of man below; but we are not to confuse this receptivity with mere passivity: the *fiat* is a positive act of will, and so the cripple is asked, 'Do you truly *want* to be cured?', and his reply acknowledges his need of help if he is to get down into the waters at that creative moment of genesis when the waters are 'stirred up' in the chaos which precedes the emergence of form: then, because of that declaration of the need and the desire to be helped, his malformation can be cured and he can achieve integration, his 'wholeness of body' can be restored.

But faith involves mind as well as will; it is no use desiring integrity unless we have some grasp of what true integrity means, and we shall never have this true insight if we 'think always according to the flesh, not the spirit'. It is this carnal, materialist thinking which our Lord rebukes after his next sign, the feeding of the five thousand. Many of the universal symbols of rebirth find a place in this story: the sea journey, the climbing of the hillside, the abundance of green grass,[1] the loaves and fishes and the boy who brings them,[2] the kingship-theme (here doubly ironical inasmuch as the crowd both misunderstand the nature of the messianic kingship and also want to make a king of their King); then the withdrawal of Jesus (a feature of the journey which the mystics have so often described in terms of 'aridity' and the 'dark night of the soul'), the coming of darkness, the strong wind, the rough sea and the disciples' terror—but Jesus is master of the dark waters, walking upon them, as later he is still master even on the cross: *regnavit a ligno Deus*, God exercising his kingly rule from the tree; for his dark journey is not, like ours, undergone of necessity as the only means of attaining life, but is freely chosen *propter nos et propter nostram salutem*: 'I lay down my life . . . of

[1] A plant or a green (or golden) bough is often, as symbol of life-renewal, the object of the mythic hero's underworld quest: e.g. the submarine plant in the Gilgamesh epic or the dark vine of the abyss which was the Babylonian tree of life; and cp. the green olive branch, brought by the dove, in the story of Noah, or the green palm branches of Christ's entry into Jerusalem, as also all the biblical imagery which has reference to the paradise-garden and the tree of life, and especially, in *John*, the two gardens of the agony and the resurrection.

[2] Christ himself is both the divine *Ichthys* or Fish, and the divine fulfilment of the *Puer Aeternus* or Eternal Child symbol of which we have already encountered one example in the person of Daniel. In general, the fish symbolizes the birth or renewal of life through water; the child, often found in association with the paradise-garden or the sea, symbolizes immortal youth, freedom, and child-wisdom as opposed to worldly experience, shrewdness and calculation. But both these symbols have an immensely rich background, too complex to be discussed here since they are not among the principal symbols used by John, though the fish-symbol is prominent in the last chapter of the gospel.

my own accord: . . . I have the power to lay it down, the power to take it up again' (11^{17-18}).

The five loaves and the two fishes together make up the symbolic seven denoting completeness, in this case the complete transfiguring process wrought through the christian *mystērion* or *sacramentum*; and the fish-symbol, by combining the two ideas of baptismal waters and eucharistic food, underlines for us the unity of that *sacramentum*, the Mystery of the Cross, in its sevenfold application. But in the symbol-language of humanity the number five itself (here, the five loaves, the five thousand people) often seems to symbolize the 'natural' man as opposed to the 'spiritual' or ideal man symbolized by quaternity, the 'flesh' (*sarx*) as opposed to spirit (*pneuma*). Matter, and in particular the flesh, are God's handiwork and therefore good in themselves; but the world of *sarx* is a fallen world, twisted and crippled and sick, needing to be restored to wholeness by the power from on high; the incarnation is the descent of the heavenly Man into the world of *sarx* in order to empower earthly man to be born anew from on high and enter the world of spirit; but matter cannot thus be raised up and hallowed, man in his psychophysical totality cannot be born anew, if he himself opposes and defeats his transfiguration by his own materialism, and this is exactly what the five thousand do. Jesus tells them not to put a 'carnal' interpretation upon his words, which 'are spirit'; he tells them 'the lifeless flesh is of no avail'; he asks them, if this doctrine is a stumbling-block to them, what they will make of the far greater scandal (to carnal eyes) of his being lifted up—

for their carnal eyes will fail to see that the lifting up, in death and ascension, is both the supreme vindication of Christ himself and the proof that in his eucharistic doctrine he is indeed speaking 'according to the spirit'; but his words cannot convince them, for they 'lack the faith to hear them', and so they turn away from him, many of them, and will 'have no more to do with him' (6^{62-7}).

Our Lord had begun by speaking of the living bread, coming down from heaven, and had told them that this bread was his flesh which they must eat if they would have immortal life; and these words led them to 'argue hotly' among themselves. 'How can this man give us his flesh to eat?' they asked. But then he went on to speak not only of eating his flesh but of drinking his blood, and to this they reacted more strongly, they were outraged: 'This is a strange, crude doctrine', they say: 'who could bring himself to accept it?' The explanation of this difference is to be found in the Old Testament, and it is of great significance.

For the Hebrews, blood was *tabu*; and it was *tabu* because it was identified with the vital principle, the soul. So we read in *Deuteronomy* 12^{23}: 'Beware thou eat not the blood, for the blood is the soul, and the soul must not be eaten with the flesh but must be poured out on the ground like water'. But if we see the eucharistic doctrine not with carnal eyes but with spiritual, it must evoke a reaction very different from horror. The basic idea expressed by the shedding of blood in the ritual of sacrifice is not the taking of life but the giving of it, and the purpose of the giving is precisely that life may thereby be

preserved or renewed; and in the completion and fulfilment of this symbolism in the incarnate Word the life
thus received is the new life from on high, the new birth
in the Spirit. John tells us in his first epistle that we have
on earth a threefold witness to Christ, spirit (*pneuma*),
water, and blood, and that 'these three are one' (5[8]); for
all three signify the life-principle—the breath of life, the
living and life-giving water, the life-blood—and in the
context of the divine gift of life immortal and eternal all
three are brought together in the coming of the life-
giving Spirit after (and because of) the shedding of
Christ's blood and the flowing of blood and water from
his side. Moreover the first coming of the Spirit is in the
pentecostal wind and fire; and blood is associated with
fire, for both are 'fashioned warm and ruddy', as well as
with wine. Thus blood symbolizes not just life but life in
its fullness, 'rich and abounding': the inspiring breath,
the energizing wind, the exhilarating wine, the 'en-
thusing' fire;[1] the eucharistic discourse is linked up with
the joy of Cana, and both together point onwards to
the hour of the Son's glory (the wedding feast took place
'on the third day') and thence to the sacramental
re-presentation of that hour in the Mass, the christian
passover (the miracle of the bread took place just
before the feast of the passover, as did the cleansing of the
old temple and the announcement of the coming of the
new).

[1] This is the main reason why I have translated the *Verbum caro
factum est* of 1[14] as 'The Word became human flesh and blood'.
(To be 'enthused' means literally to be *entheos*, God-filled.)

The Mass is both *deipnon*, sacred meal, and *thysia*, sacrifice, the food eaten being the sacrificed victim; and its sacrificial aspect, its showing forth of the death and the rising again of Christ, is conveyed to us through the symbolic 'separation' and then re-uniting or 'commingling' of the Body and the Blood. The identification of 'blood' with 'soul' or 'life-principle' makes this symbolism much clearer and more meaningful for us: the Old Testament injunction is now reversed: we *are* to eat the flesh with the soul, for the food offered is the living Bread, the living Christ, and the drink offered (as our Lord will later declare, 7[38-9]) is the 'living water' by which he means 'the Spirit'—so that here again - Spirit and water and blood are one.

7. *Blindness and Judgement*

By the time our Lord makes this last declaration the darkness is beginning to close in on him: the opposition of the Jews[1] has hardened and grown more bitter; interruptions when he speaks are becoming frequent; the chief priests and pharisees have tried to arrest him, and some among

[1] By 'the Jews' John means the official leaders of Judaism, whose headquarters were in Jerusalem, and those who joined with them in opposing our Lord and finally in bringing about his trial and death. We sometimes need to remind ourselves that 'the Jews' in this sense are *not* the people of Israel as a whole (any more than the 'Greeks' of 12[20] are people of Greek race), and that Jesus himself and his mother and foster-father, his friends and his first followers, are all Jews.

the crowd have wanted to seize hold of him. And so, by the march of events as well as by the unfolding of Christ's doctrine, we are led on to a discussion of the second and greater obstacle in the way of receiving the light and the life: the sort of blindness which is incurable inasmuch as it is wilful, born not just of ignorance and stupidity, as 'carnal thinking' might be, but of pride and complacency: not just a failure but a refusal to see the light, a repudiation of the light. For this sort of blindness, therefore, the coming of the light into the world is in itself a judgement on the world: it is the moment of crisis, of *krisis*, of decision, in which sentence is passed on the world by the world itself.

There are two points here of capital importance. Every man must be judged; on every man sentence must be passed—of life or death eternal. But, first, we are not to think of this judgement merely as an event in some remote eschatological future; and secondly we are not to think of it at all as an unpredictable or arbitrary sentence. To say that we are to be judged means in effect that we are to judge ourselves; and the judgement is not something we may have chosen to think or say about ourselves, it is quite simply what we have chosen to be. The sentence is a statement of fact; the Day of Judgement is the solemn declaration of that fact: we either have or have not become children of the light, living in the light, we are or are not children of the sun, able because of our solar nature to walk free and unharmed in the sun because fire is our element. As the one work demanded of us is faith (6^{29}), and the one command given us is love

($15^{12, 17}$), so the one unforgivable—that is, incurable—sin is the chosen and cherished blindness of those who knowingly and wilfully repudiate the light because they are too proud to confess their blindness and therefore when confronted with the light deny its existence. This is the 'blasphemy against the holy Spirit' of *Matthew* 12^{32}, the sin of denying or repudiating the known truth, knowing that black is black and yet calling it white because (as Christ said of Satan) to speak falsehood is but to speak one's own idiom (*Jn.* 8^{44}).

This explains the paradox of 3^{17} and 9^{39}, our Lord's assertion, first that he has not come to judge the world, and then that his Father has left all judgement to him (5^{22}) and his coming does mean judging the world: his *purpose* in coming was not to judge, i.e. to condemn, but to save; but the *effect* of his coming is to bring a judgement, i.e. to precipitate a *krisis*, a decision: confronted with the light, men must either accept or repudiate the light, must either give or withhold their faith; those who accept the light cannot be condemned, for in accepting they have already passed from death into life (5^{24}); those who reject the light are already condemned, for to reject the light is to condemn themselves to darkness: they make darkness their native land as they make falsehood their native tongue. So, Christ says, his coming into the world must bring a judgement on the world since 'those who humbly confess their blindness are given sight; those who pride themselves on their vision become yet blinder than before': they 'claim to see clearly' and therefore they cannot escape their sin, they make it immovable and

'so must die' in it, their 'sin of rejecting me now'
($9^{39, 41}$; 8^{24}).

The discussion of blindness thus involves an elucidation of the true nature of sin, which in turn involves
elucidating the true nature of law. This discussion is of
course most immediately linked with the sign of the
blind man; but its main themes are already evident in
the sign of the cripple; and in both cases the focal point
of conflict is the breaking of the sabbath.

The cripple cannot himself achieve wholeness: it must
be given him; but once it is given he must carry his own
bed and make his own way, his own journey, and our
Lord tells him clearly what the journey essentially involves: 'Now that you are made whole again in body,
keep yourself from sin' (5^{14}). But according to the Jews
he had already sinned: he had broken the sabbath; and
Christ's warning against sin, following at once on their
accusation, is an implicit—but dramatically striking—
condemnation of their legalist misunderstanding of what
sin is. This he goes on to make explicit: 'Moses gave you
the law, but you do not keep the truth of the law'
(7^{19}), and so it is Moses himself, 'the man in whom you
put your trust' who 'is your accuser' (5^{45}). And the accusation is not that they are too zealous in keeping the sabbath or the law in general but on the contrary that they
are destroying the truth of the law and the sabbath,
destroying the peace of the sabbath with their sabba-
tarianism and killing the law with their legalism.

Legalism kills law by perverting its nature and pre-
venting a true understanding of it, turning a free and

loving service into a blind and fettered superstition. Hence it is with a denial of the Jews' superstitious theory of guilt and punishment that the sign of the blind man begins. Our Lord repudiates this theory;[1] and then he goes back to the beginning, back to the first genesis of man: the clay made with spittle recalls the aboriginal slime from which man was fashioned, and, as it was in the beginning, the living eyes are rubbed in by the sculptor's thumbs; the waters of the pool, stirred up when the man washes—as the cripple's pool was stirred up by each fresh inflow of water from the source[2]—recall the waters of primordial chaos. But the name of this pool means 'one who is sent', the living water, light-giving, sight-giving, is the christian *mystērion*, the sacramental Christ, prefigured in those Jordan-waters in which Naaman the leper was sent to wash seven times, whereupon his flesh became 'as the flesh of a little child' (IV *Kings*, 5[14]).

Rightly understood, God's law is living and life-giving because it is identical with the Way, the Truth, the Word, the Water. The legalist dislikes the idea of living water or living words: they are too fluid and unpredictable, too mercurial, they may so easily escape his control: he feels he is far safer dealing with the rigid immobility of a cadaver than with the quick flesh of a little child. But the Law cannot be killed, because it is the eternal light and

[1] He does not of course deny that pain and suffering in general are caused by moral evil: on the contrary: cf. *infra*, pp. 83–4.

[2] The reference to an angel stirring up the waters (5[4]) is absent from the best MSS and is usually regarded as an interpolation; a natural explanation of the phenomenon is offered e.g. by Lagrange, *Evang.s.S.Jean*, pp. 134–5.

life; it will not conform to the legalist's lifeless categories precisely because it is the 'Mercurial', the life-bringing, Water; it cannot be equated with a merely external correctitude because it is the living pattern of Love.

Lex tua veritas: the law *is* the Truth, the living Word: it is not just a law promulgated by Christ, it is Christ. Morality therefore consists, not in being conformed to the rigidity of a lifeless code, but in being transformed into the likeness of the living Word; it consists essentially in the imitation of Christ, in becoming assimilated to, and living in, Christ; it is essentially a religious dialogue, a communion, in which man lovingly (and therefore freely) gives back to God the life and the love which God has given him.

It may be useful to distinguish here two pairs of contrasting ideas, closely related but by no means identical, with which the gospel presents us. The first contrast is that between the 'law given to man by Moses' and the 'life, gracious and true, brought to man by Christ' (1^{17}). The relationship between the two terms is that of imperfect to perfect: the old law (which Christ came 'not to destroy but to fulfil') is brought to its fulfilment in the new; and the fulfilment concerns both the content of the law and man's attitude to it.

The content is changed inasmuch as the minimal negative requirements of justice or righteousness are now to be seen in the setting of the positive ideal of *caritas*: so, for instance, the prohibition of murder contrasts with the statement of the love which makes a man ready to give his life for his friend.

The attitude is changed inasmuch as the old law was written on tablets of stone, the new law is inscribed in the heart; the old law was essentially external to man, it indicated what was right without giving man the power to do what was right—hence St Paul's insistence on the close relationship between law (in this sense) and sin, and on the idea of the law as a 'bondage'—whereas the new law is essentially internal, as life is internal, it consists essentially in the identifying of our will with the will of God, and therefore in escaping from bondage not by repudiating the law (which would mean falling into the worse bondage of sin) but by internalizing it, seeing it and accepting it as the pattern of life and completeness and fulfilment for us and therefore willing to make it our own—which means, in one word, willing to live in Love.

The second contrast is that between legalism and the free and gracious living of the truth of the law; and here there can be no question of making perfect what was imperfect, for legalism is not imperfect, it is basically wrong, and here therefore it would be proper to say that Christ came not to fulfil but to destroy. Legalism is carnal thinking; its concern is with the dead letter as opposed to the living spirit, the living truth, of the law; its only concern is with a dead and death-bringing code (death-bringing because static, with the *stasis* of death) for it has no understanding of the *dynamism* of law-as-life: it cannot see for instance how individual positive laws are always to be viewed in function of the total pattern; it can only see the letter of each individual law, and consequently it will often, through adhering to the letter, sin against the spirit. (So the legalist of today will have a guilt-sense about not going to church on Sunday even though, because of illness or some overriding duty of justice or charity, he is quite unable to do so: he has not conformed to the letter, and that is as far as he can see.)

There is thus an irremediable opposition not merely between legalism and life but between legalism and law in the true sense of the word. But between law and life there is no opposition—on the contrary, the two are identical—if law is rightly understood, and accepted and treasured in the heart, as being the way to life because it is the way of Life.

Accepting the law in one's heart, however, does not necessarily mean always living in accordance with the law in practice: as long as we remain in our state of disintegration we find ourselves constantly torn in different directions, willing one thing and doing another, wanting to do what we know to be right but in our weakness failing to do it. Nevertheless there is a world of difference between this sort of failure and the sins which are a deliberate repudiation of the way and the truth. *The Cloud of Unknowing* tells us: 'Not what thou art nor what thou hast been, seeth God with his merciful eyes, but what thou wouldest be'. To say that our law is Christ is to say that sin is essentially not a transgression against a rule (as it is for the legalist) but a rebellion against a person, against the Word who is Love; and so 'in the end we shall be judged on love' because the essential malice of sin consists in a refusal to return love for love. This explains our Lord's attitude to sin: his assertion that the 'harlots and sinners' are the first to enter the kingdom, and his gentleness with human weakness; on the other hand his anger at pride and self-righteousness, at the impiety which defiles his Father's temple and the black-heartedness which knows neither sorrow for its own sin nor pity for the weaknesses of others. It explains also the growing fury of the Jews against this sabbath-breaker who not only swept aside contemptuously their own view of law and of sin but sharply contrasted it with the true one; a logical progression begins with their wanting to stone the poor woman caught in adultery and ends with their wanting to stone our Lord.

It is generally held that this story of the adulteress is not part of the original gospel nor from the pen of John himself; nevertheless it is incontestably, in the catholic view, part of the canon of the inspired scriptures; and if we put it with the stories of the wedding and the temple-cleansing we find that this triad of incidents gives us a complete picture of the christian evaluation both of material things and of the sins they can occasion, while at the same time this third story forms a sharp contrast with our Lord's treatment of the very different sin of proud and wilful blindness. (I have in fact ventured to transfer the story from the beginning of the eighth chapter to the end, partly because this avoids interrupting the development of our Lord's thought, but partly also because in this way it leads straight into the sign of the blind man.)

Material things are good in themselves; they are good for us if kept in their right place, and their right place is the framework of the divine way; if we fail to keep them in their place—if we value, love, use, enjoy them in the wrong manner or degree—we sin. Our Lord does not deny the woman's sin; on the contrary, by implication he affirms it when he tells her not to sin again. Nor is he minimizing its gravity when he declares that he will not condemn her: he is but repeating what we were told before (3^{17}), that he was sent 'not to condemn the world but to save the world'.

But if our Lord affirms by implication the reality of the woman's sin, he also by implication affirms the far greater gravity of the sin of those who self-righteously condemned her. To be wilfully blind and in one's blindness to pride oneself on one's clarity of vision is to be incapable of seeing the truth, however obvious it may be: 'That is what is so amazing,' the blind man tells them, 'that you should have no idea where he came from and yet he opened my eyes' (9^{30}). To blind one's eyes to the sight of the Sun, to shut one's ears to the sound of the Word, this is the essential sin, the essential rebellion, because this and only this means a deliberate refusal to be a child of the light and a deliberate choosing instead to be a child of the dark mystery of iniquity whose idiom is falsehood (8^{43-4}).

8. *Life and Death in Combat*

It seems reasonable to suppose that it was the thought of that mystery of iniquity as the primary cause of the appalling burden of misery and evil which weighs down the world—the sadness of its pain and mortality and decay, the far greater tragedy of the blindness of heart, the evil stupidity, which makes us reject life and wholeness and happiness—that aroused our Lord's anger during the sign of Lazarus.

Just before this we have had the tenderness of the *paroimia* of the sheepfold, with its echoes of one of the best loved of the psalms, 'The Lord is my shepherd: how shall I want for anything? He gives me a resting-place where there are green pastures; he leads me to the cool waters, that I may be refreshed and live anew' (*Ps.* 22$^{1, 2}$). Christ is the door of the sheepfold: those who enter therein will be safe and sound; Christ is the good shepherd who lays down his life for his sheep, who knows them, lovingly, each of them by name, and they follow him when he calls them because they know his voice (cf. 10$^{9, 11, 14, 3}$). But the *paroimia* causes a fresh outburst of discord among the Jews; some accuse our Lord of madness or diabolic possession; and when he returns to the theme during the feast of the dedication of the temple and declares that his sheep are safe in his hands for ever— no power can snatch them from him, for he has his Father's power to defend them since he and the Father

ST. JOSEPH'S NOVITIATE
BAILEYS HARBOR, WISCONSIN

are one—then in a fury they take up stones to kill him (10²⁷⁻³⁰).

The message then comes from Martha and Mary, 'Your friend is ill' (11³). The structure of this Lazarus story is markedly antiphonal: a constant alternation of tender, human, gentle things with the starkness and ugliness of our human situation symbolized by the stinking corpse[1]—it is the fourth day since the burial, not the third. Our Lord, having delayed his departure for two days, then tells his disciples they are going back to Judaea and they are horrified, reminding him that the Jews want to stone him to death; but his answer ('In the day's course there are but twelve hours of daylight'[2]) sounds the same note of urgency that is in his words at Sichar—the fields already ripe for the harvesting, no four months' interval between sowing and reaping—and in the sign of the blind man—the imminent coming of the night, when one can work no longer. At the same time his words can be read as a re-assurance; there is no immediate danger for him, for his 'hour of darkness' has not yet come, nor for them, since men can walk safely as long as 'the world's light' is with them.

There follows immediately the reference to Lazarus as having fallen asleep. This identification of death with sleep has already been mentioned in the context of our Lord's own death (cf. *supra*, p. 59); in the synoptics his

[1] *The Cloud of Unknowing* speaks of the ego as a 'stinking lump'.
[2] The day, sunrise to sunset, was divided into twelve equal periods or 'hours'. Metaphorically, the day's course signifies a man's life-span; nightfall, death, puts a stop to his activity, his life-work.

use of similar language ('The girl is not dead, but asleep') causes the onlookers to jeer at him (*Mt.* 9[24]); the liturgy of the Mass, speaking in paradox as Christ did, describes the souls in the purifying crucible of fire as sleeping the sleep of peace. In the Lazarus story this identification is emphasized by the paradox in our Lord's first words: 'This illness is not to end in death'.

Christians can and do feel the fear of death, the terror of dying, as much as other men, just as they feel the loss of those they love as much as other men. But when it is a question not of feeling but of thought they should be in very different case from those who have no hope in a future life and for whom death means final extinction. The christian should be able to face the thought of death with equanimity precisely because it is like the sleep which closes one day and leads on into another: it is a moment of transition, a *transitus*, from one world to another, greater world, and primitive peoples who exorcize death of its fears by treating it as a *rite de passage* express thereby a profound even though dim or distorted insight which is found purified and illumined, and strengthened by the firmness of faith and hope, in the christian prayers for a 'departing soul'.

In one sense therefore the moment of death should seem of far less importance to the christian than to the non-believer. But in another sense it must be of far greater importance, since it is the moment of ultimate *krisis* or decision upon which eternity hangs: we pass judgement upon ourselves, and this is the moment at which sentence is definitively pronounced. Yet here again

we are not to confuse religion with superstition: we are
not to suppose that after a lifetime of truly loving and
devoted service of God a man could in his last moments
slip into some contravention of the law which would
nullify all his love and his goodness and plunge him into
hell. We shall die as we have lived—we shall be, when
death comes, what our way of life has made us—but with
one qualification of immense importance: it is superstition to suppose that a lifetime of love can be wiped out
by a moment of frailty; it is not superstition to believe
that a lifetime of frailty can be redeemed by a moment of
love, for our Lord, in his words to the 'good thief'[1] and
his comment on the woman 'who was a sinner', tells us
that this is so. Jesus is the Lord of life, physical and
spiritual, temporal and eternal; and when he speaks to
Martha of life and death it is with the life eternal that he
is concerned. Martha's appeal for his help has been
couched in vague terms: she has not formulated to her-
self the possibility of his raising Lazarus from the dead;
when he tells her, 'Your brother will rise again', she
thinks he is referring to the resurrection at the end of the
world; and even when he goes on to declare that he is
resurrection, here and now, because he is life, he still
does not announce his immediate purpose, the 'sign', but
states the ultimate reality to which that sign points: that
those who believe in him shall never die, for already,
here and now, they have triumphed over death in every
sense of the word that really matters.

[1] This expression epitomizes our Lord's denunciations of legalism:
in the eyes of the legalist there can be no such thing.

Thus the series of *sēmeia* reaches the climax towards which they have been progressively mounting: the explicit meeting of Life and death, the definitive victory of Life over death.[1] But now in this moment of triumphant announcement, Mary comes to him and falls at his feet, weeping; and Jesus is 'deeply troubled in spirit', so that he groans 'from grief and anger'. We are justified in interpreting this verb, *embrimasthai*, as meaning intense anger as well as grief, since this accords with biblical usage elsewhere; but what is the cause of the anger? It is hardly plausible to see it as due simply to the inadequacy of faith and insight shown by those around our Lord, just as his intense grief can hardly be due simply to the death of his friend (for he had purposely postponed his coming till after Lazarus was dead). But if we reflect that our Lord's gaze was directed not only at the sign but at what it signified, not only at the immediate circumstances, the physical death and the tears shed for it, but at the infinitely greater tragedy of spiritual death, the infinitely greater horror of the evil which causes it and thereby causes also the immensity of the world's pain, the *lacrimae rerum*, the tears with which the whole world is drenched; and if we add to this our Lord's awareness that this sign would precipitate the final attack upon himself and so bring about his own death, and that when he was

---

[1] In the first of the healing signs the open conflict between life and death is already implicit: the literal meaning of our Lord's words of re-assurance to the nobleman is 'Your son lives', and it was with these words that Elijah restored to the widow of Sarephta her son whom he had brought back to life (III *Kings*, 17[23]).

lifted up there would be some who would gaze at him, not lovingly, to receive life, but jeering at him in a final act of life-rejection—if we bear all this in mind it is indeed not unreasonable to suppose, as was suggested above, that our Lord's intense anger was directed against the dark mystery of evil—soon, now, to be referred to as the 'Prince of this world' (12^{31})—who is responsible in the last resort for all the vileness and treachery and cruelty, all the blindness and folly and futility, and all the appalling pain and misery, which darken the lives and the hearts of men.

The sign of Lazarus does in fact produce a quickening of the pace of events: a meeting of the Sanhedrin is called; Caiphas prophesies; the Jews plot how to kill Jesus; he hides himself from them in the countryside on the edge of the desert; the anointing of his feet by Mary symbolically announces his burial; the chief priests plot to kill Lazarus also; and then Jesus makes his triumphal entry into Jerusalem, and with the unconscious irony so characteristic of this gospel the pharisees cry out in desperation that 'the whole world is going over to him' (12^{19})—and at this point Jesus is told that some Greeks are asking if they may speak to him.

Hellēnes as used here means, not people who are Greek by birth, but either Gentiles or else Greek-speaking Jews of the Diaspora: their coming—which recalls the unconscious irony of an earlier question: 'Will he go to . . . teach the Greeks?' (7^{35})—marks the end of our Lord's ministry to the Palestinian Jews, since they have now finally rejected him,[1] and announces the universal apostolate, the teaching of all nations, which is to come. Symbolically, the aptness of the term 'Greeks' is obvious, and links this scene with the story of the Magi: the 'Jews' have so distorted the revealed truth given them in the Old Testament that when the Truth comes amongst them they turn him away, and in so doing they deny not only the divinity of the Truth but their own humanity: their life-refusal makes them less than human. By contrast, the natural wisdom of man is drawn to the Truth—'when I am lifted up I will draw all men to myself' (12^{32})—for naturalness and humanness have more affinity with the Truth than has a perversion of religion.

It is significant that the two disciples who play a part in this incident have Greek names: first, they are as it were the heralds of this announcement of the universal apostolate; secondly they stand in sharp contrast to 'the Jews' who were the implacable enemies of Christ and of his gospel. These latter, despite the knowledge of God revealed to them by God, brought *against* Christ the obstruction of their dead legalism; whereas the natural wisdom represented by 'Greeks' and Magi brought gifts *to* Christ, nature offering itself in sacrifice to God that God might hallow nature. The Magi offered the gold of their kingship to the Sun-King that human authority might be hallowed and mellowed by sharing in Christ's solar nature; they offered the incense of priesthood that priesthood might be a true mediation, not an attempted Promethean stealth but a God-given bringing of Fire to

[1] cf. *supra*, p. 69n.

85

men; they offered myrrh in acceptance of the fact that life is attained through death and wisdom is attained through humility, not hubris, and that the 'dry bones' of all natural human endeavour must be brought to Life in order to be brought to life.

Our Lord makes no direct reply to the Greeks' message, but his next words acknowledge its significance: 'So has the hour come for the Son of Man to be glorified' (12^{23}); he goes on to speak of the dark journey, his and ours, in terms of the grain of wheat buried in the ground; and then, refusing despite his distress of spirit to pray to be saved from this his hour he prays instead: 'Father, make known your glory'—and one is tempted to write 'Glory', here as in the prologue, for there follows Christ's declaration, authenticated by the voice from heaven, that when he is lifted up he will draw all men to himself; but the primary meaning is clearly a re-assertion of his desire to do the will of his Father in this his hour, and so, as always, to glorify his Father.

And still the Jews persist in their blindness and their rejection of life, as little affected by the voice from heaven as they have been by all the words and works of Jesus; and now, in the account of the last supper, we are shown in the person of Judas a terrifying picture of how rejection can finally become immovable, irremediable: already beforehand he had allowed his heart to listen to Satan's voice, but now, when he takes the morsel of food from Jesus (a gesture of friendship and fellowship akin to the kiss recorded by the synoptics), he is finally, decisively committed to evil, and Satan enters into him.

The greatness of his sin is dramatically emphasized by contrast with its setting, the supper-table, the *agapē*, the beloved disciple leaning back on Jesus' breast, and above all Jesus himself wanting to prove to 'those he was leaving behind him . . . how boundlessly he loved them' and so taking on himself 'the appearance and office of a slave' and humbly washing their feet (cf. 13^1 *sqq.*).

9. *The Man of Sorrows*

This active assumption, by him who is Lord and Master, of the exactly opposite role of slave is an implicit assertion that when in the course of the Passion words, actions, situations, express—but in the blasphemy of scorn and mockery—a similar reversal of roles, or, as in the crowning with thorns, a travesty of his own true role, these humiliations are not forced on him against his will but are freely chosen by him for the fulfilling of the scriptures, of the whole cosmic process, of man's eternal destiny.

We may think of the *kenōsis* of the Word, his emptying himself of his glory, as comprising three moments, three progressive degrees of lowliness: his acceptance, first, of our creaturely human condition; secondly, of the 'appearance and office of a slave' at the maundy; thirdly, of the humiliations to which he allows himself to be subjected during his Passion. In the same way we may think of him as accepting and undergoing a threefold *descensus*, a progressive lowliness not in himself, in his own 'status', but in his circumstances: first, the poverty of his life, both as child and as man; secondly, the human squalors from which he did not hold himself aloof but into which he willingly entered, for he came to redeem us not merely from our squalors but in our squalors; thirdly, the ugliness and horror of the circumstances of Passion and death, and the final pitiful crudity of burial in the tomb.

It is the second *descensus* which concerns us here. He suffered himself to be 'despised and rejected' by men; but he himself would not despise or reject either humanity in general or in particular the company of the dull and stupid and squalid, the outcasts, the lepers, the 'harlots and sinners'. He turned away only where he was turned away: from the proud and self-righteous. This fact takes us further and deeper into the conflict between our Lord and the legalists. The ultimate ethical concepts are not right and wrong but good and evil: an action which is objectively wrong may, if it comes of an inculpably mistaken judgement and is motivated by a truly generous and selfless love, be an act of high and even heroic virtue; an objectively right action which is an expression simply of pride or jealousy or blackhearted malice will be gravely sinful. The Jewish legalists were concerned with right and wrong, with the letter of the law; our Lord was of course concerned with the objective standards of right and wrong ('If you love me, keep my commandments') but was far more concerned with the far deeper issue of good and evil—the 'one commandment' he left his disciples was the commandment of love.

But the division is wider even than that: the legalists, being self-righteous literalists, were sectaries of the cult of conventionality, of respectability; like the *bien-pensants* of all times their only standard of conduct was what is *correct* (in the French sense) and they were ready to damn out of hand and to excommunicate anyone who failed to conform to this standard. But our Lord was not conventional; he was not respectable in the worldly sense of the word. In his world and his heart there were no 'untouchables'. The artist can discern beauty in a huddle of mean streets and hovels; the saint can see in them the sorrow and love of God. The woman of whom our Lord said that many sins were forgiven her because of the greatness of her love was a prostitute. There is a universe of difference between 'sinners' and sinners. Bernanos said, 'Hell is not to love any more': it is the self-righteous pillars of respectability, in their ivory tower of pride, who by definition cannot love.

Christ was unconventional; as Lagrange pointed out, even today in Palestine it is quite contrary to custom, if one meets a woman on the road or by a well, to enter into conversation with her. Hence the surprise of the disciples on their return from the city (4²⁷).

Christ was not 'respectable'; his kindness and sympathy were clearly shown to the scandalous *adultera*, not to the respectable people who wanted to stone her; and it seems reasonable enough to regard his long conversation with the woman at Sichar as being far from 'respectable' since, quite apart from being a Samaritan and therefore anathema to good, respectable Jews, she seems to have been a somewhat dubious character. There are allegorical interpretations of the five husbands and the sixth man who was not a husband, but they strike one as being a little far-fetched and they are certainly unnecessary: there is ample point to the story if we take the situation quite literally: it seems clear enough that her private life had not been a model of tidiness and conventional rectitude; and the symbolism of the numbers, five for the 'carnal' as against the 'spiritual' man, and six as signifying the 'imperfect', is surely apt enough.

If this interpretation is valid we have to notice once again that our Lord does not treat this kind of sin as negligible: on the contrary, it is when she asks him for the water which only he can give her that he introduces the subject, the implication being that we are not capable of receiving this water unless we are willing to 'abandon the ways of darkness' and to make a fresh beginning, to 'put on the armour of light' (*Rom.* 13^{12}). But the fact remains that it is to this woman in all her unworthiness that he addresses his lovely words about the living water: for always his love descends into our squalors to search for the one sinner as against the ninety-nine just, for the prodigal son as against his respectable brother, for the lost sheep, the outcast, for all who are most in need of love.

And so we return to the maundy. It is 'the eve of the pasch'. They have sat down to supper. Jesus lays aside his clothes, and washes their feet. In biblical usage the literal sense of 'naked' is often 'without one's outer garments'; symbolically the term refers us back to the figure of the *puer aeternus*;[1] here, as also later in the Passion when Jesus is 'stripped of his garments', what the symbol conveys to us is the recovery of the youthful vitality, the freedom, the joy of the child *through* the *kenōsis*— the standing before God in poverty and nakedness—of the man; and this idea of the humble reversal of the original arrogant falsehood is carried forward in the maundy, the washing. This is 'not for a cleansing', for they are 'already wholly clean'; and they are wholly clean, as Jesus will explain later (15[3]) because of 'the words I have spoken to you, the words which are life for you': for the Word is the Fire, the Sun, and therefore to hear the Word in one's heart is to be burned clean of all impurity (in the proper sense of the word: all the dross of falsehood, all that prevents integrity) by the Fire. The purpose of the maundy, our Lord explains, is to show them that the truth, the essence, alike of love and of the law lies in humble self-giving.

Ruysbroeck's saying, 'Be kind, be kind, and you will be saints' can mean either 'If you are always kind you will end by being holy' or 'If you are always kind, this shows that you are already holy': kindness is a means to holiness, it is also the constant inevitable overflow of holiness—or wholeness—and in fact it is only in the latter sense that the full glory of *caritas* will be found. The false 'charity' which springs from pride and expresses condescension is not kindness at all; the kindness which springs from a sense of duty and is therefore rather laboured, perhaps rather impersonal, is a means to

[1] cf. *The Paradise Tree*, pp. 34 *sqq.*

perfection but is as yet far from being itself the perfection of *caritas*; but the kindness St Paul speaks of when he tells us that 'love is kind' is perfect kindness because it is the expression and overflow of wholeness, and so it has in it the lovely freshness and spontaneity and the deeply personal quality of the kindness of the saints. A saint is never kind to a sinner: he is always kind to *this* sinner. So the narrative goes on to mention the 'disciple whom Jesus loved', 'leaning back on Jesus' breast', and then to the announcement of the 'new commandment': 'Love one another as I have loved you' (13^{34}).

In what sense is this a new commandment? For it had been said to them of old, Thou shalt love thy neighbour as thyself (*Levit.* 19^{18}). The answer lies in the idea of 'interinanimation': 'I live in my Father and you live in me and I in you' (14^{20}) is followed by 'As the Father has loved me, so I have loved you: live, then, in my love' (15^{9}) and by the whole *paroimia* of the vine and the branches: 'You will live in my love if you obey the commands I have given you', for 'if you do as I command you', 'you are my friends' (15$^{10, 14}$); and this in turn leads on to the re-statement of the new commandment in terms of the man who 'gives his life for the friends he loves' (15^{13}).

The new law does therefore go beyond the old inasmuch as, since the new law *is* Christ, the love enjoined by it is the imitation of Christ's love, a love which is self-sacrificial. Such a love is no easy matter, as we know to our cost: it can spring only from interinanimation: the mutual indwelling represented by the beloved disciple at

the supper is contrasted not only with the treachery of
Judas but with the too facile declaration of Peter that he
is ready to die for Jesus (13^{37}): it must be learnt through
the labours of the dark journey, the humble docility of
kenōsis, the emptying of the self of all falsehood (and
therefore of all pride) so as to be able to hear the voice of
the indwelling Spirit, the Paraclete.

The word *paraclētos* means first of all a legal assistant,
an advocate, a defending counsel; but it also means one
who speaks out prophetically, proclaiming, exhorting,
enlightening; and this leads to a third meaning, one who
consoles, when the message proclaimed is the message of
salvation, of hope and of joy. In the first epistle of St John
(2^1) our Lord is referred to as a paraclete or advocate who
will plead our cause; and this is implicitly affirmed by
Christ himself when he tells the disciples he will send
them another paraclete to befriend and defend them.
But there is an essential difference between the mode of
activity of the Spirit and that of the incarnate Word: the
mission of the Spirit is the direct result of the mission of
the Son: the lifting up of the Son in death and glory
brings about the coming down of the pentecostal wind
and fire (and thus the essential pattern of sacrifice is fulfilled; for sacrifice, like morality, is *dialogal* in structure);
but the Spirit does not simply continue the work of the
Son; his activity is of a different kind precisely because it
is the activity of spirit whereas the work of the Son was
carried out through his human flesh. So our Lord taught
the multitudes, but it was as one man teaching another,
through the medium of human speech which is addressed

to the ear and thence the brain but may fail to penetrate the depths of the personality, to reach the heart. The Spirit will not teach men what they have never been taught before: he will teach them what they have been taught before but have failed to assimilate so fully as to be possessed by the truth in mind and heart alike. It is the hearts of men that the Spirit instructs; and instructs not by an external voice but by his indwelling presence, by being for them precisely the breath of life.

This knowledge, then, is love-knowledge: not a cold, academic apprehension of truths but an assimilation, an affinity, a living and loving union with the truth who is also goodness and beauty and light and life and love; it is the *initia*[1] of the life which is eternal and at the same time the transfiguring process through which man is refashioned in the likeness of Love and thereby attains the joy and the peace of which our Lord now speaks: his joy, which will fill their hearts brimful; his peace, which will keep them always in good heart (cf. 15^{11}; 14^{27}).

When Jesus had finished speaking he went out with his disciples[2] into the dark night; they crossed over the brook Kedron, which means Dark Torrent, and so entered the garden of agony, the garden called Gethsemani or Oil-Press. Crossing a brook means taking some vital and hazardous decision, 'taking the plunge' and in one sense or another going into battle; so Jacob, at the last stage of

[1] i.e. the beginning of, and entry into; cf. *supra*, p. 54.
[2] I have transferred the last words of ch. 14 'Come, we must be on our way', to the beginning of ch. 18 so as to avoid interrupting our Lord's discourse.

his journey to integrity, crossed the brook Jabbok before his night-long struggle with the angel. We must not think of Kedron as a cool, refreshing stream: it is a dark ravine, arid and waterless except in the rainy seasons; often therefore it is the 'waste land' where there is

> *no water but only rock*
> *Rock and no water and the sandy road*
> *The road winding above among the mountains*
> *Which are mountains of rock without water*
> *If there were water we should stop and drink*
> *Amongst the rock one cannot stop or think*
> *Sweat is dry and feet are in the sand*
> *If there were only water amongst the rock* [1] . . .

In the same way the garden of agony contrasts with the paradise-garden: the oil is the wrestlers' oil, a preparation for the coming *agōn*; in Origen's phrase it was 'as an athlete'[2] that Christ was led by the Spirit into the wilderness to do battle with Satan before beginning his ministry; it is in the same spirit, and led by the same Spirit, that he goes now into the garden. For Kedron, Gethsemani and the hill of Golgotha stand at the mid-point of history, between the original paradise which was lost to us and the eternal paradise which was yet to be won for us, and won by bitter struggle; and if we are to attain to that second paradise we too must struggle: as William Law put it, we must cross over the brook Kedron and sweat drops of sorrow in company with Christ.

The travesty-symbols referred to at the beginning of

[1] T. S. Eliot: *The Waste Land.*   [2] *Homil. in Luc.* xxxi.

this section are thus strictly functional: as, in general, light is attained through darkness and we find life through losing it, so in particular if we are to find love in its fullness we may have to know loneliness like that of Christ in the garden; if we are to have life 'rich and abounding' we must first be stripped of possessiveness; the tree or pillar or ladder mounting to heaven may have to be, for us as for him, first of all a pillar of scourging, a tree of crucifixion; if we are to share in his kingship we must be prepared to wear a crown of thorns; if we are to be lifted up in glory and majesty we must first be lifted up in mockery or self-mockery; if we are to drink of the fruit of the vine in eternity we must first know the taste of the vinegar; and if *in novissimo die* we are to rejoice in the radiance of the risen flesh we must first know the thrust of the lance, the darkness of the tomb.

These parallelisms are in the realm of symbol: though there are indeed some among Christ's followers whose journey does closely and literally resemble his own, for the vast majority the following is undramatic, the symbols remain symbols. But a following, a sharing, a descent into darkness in one sense or another there must be, even if, as may be when God's hands are most gentle, the darkness seems more aptly described as a sleep than as a death.

John omits the account of the agony and therefore the incident of the apostles' sleeping instead of keeping watch with our Lord, though in the Last Supper discourse Christ has told them how they will all be scattered, 'each of you going his own way and leaving me quite alone'

(16^{32}). But it is important to distinguish the two different meanings of sleep as a symbol: the re-creative death-sleep out of which life springs anew, and the sterile sleep of inertia and sloth.

The Lamb of God takes on himself, and therefore 'takes away', the world's sin, and in that sense recalls and fulfills, as we have seen, the Old Testament Day of Atonement and its scapegoat. But we must not think of Christ as a scapegoat in the sense of relieving us of all responsibility and all need of action, shouldering the burden not only of the guilt of our disintegration but also of all the suffering, the darkness, which is meant on the contrary to be part of the process of our re-integration. We must not think, or behave as if we thought, that we for our part have nothing to do and nothing to suffer since all has been done for us, like those royal children who were punished by proxy for their misdemeanours thanks to the 'whipping-boys' who had to take the punishment in their stead. Christ does take on himself the burden not only of our guilt but of our suffering; but it is in order to make it possible for us to act and suffer, ourselves, in such a way as to be made whole. The unforgivable sin was described above as the incurable sin— it is unforgivable to the extent to which it is incurable— for we are not to think of forgiveness as a simple erasure, a benign decision to turn a blind eye on our sin and pretend it never happened: forgiving us means giving us back the power to act creatively, to attain integrity; it means restoring our *dynamism*; and that is why the wilful blindness of the legalists is incurable, precisely because legalism, as we have seen, is essentially *static*, and their *stasis* is stubbornly, wilfully immovable. Apart from a miracle, there is no way of turning a dead code into a vital process; and there is in the nature of things no way of recovering vitality and creative dynamism within the framework of a wilfully lifeless conformity. These dry bones shall not live because these dry bones cannot live.

Christ died for our sins that we might die to our sins. But that death is not a simple negation. To say that we must suffer death in our turn means that we must suffer the death involved in our turning again to God—in that 'conversion', that *metanoia* or change of mind and heart preached by the Baptist, which is the finding of the renewal of faith through sorrow. The christian liturgy prays constantly: *Converte nos Deus salutaris noster*, 'Turn us again to you, God our salvation', echoing such cries as that in the prophecy of Jeremiah, 'Turn me back to you and I shall be turned [converted], for you are the Lord my God' (cf. *Jer.* 31[18]): faith is a dialogue, a gift God gives us to give back to him; he turning to us, as Christ turned to the two disciples, that in so doing he may cause us to turn to him—and to turn, if need be, not once but again and again, 'seventy times seven times', till the conversion is complete, total. (Perhaps we may be allowed to see a hint of this in the repeated turning of Mary Magdalen to Christ in the resurrection-garden, 20[14, 16].)

The *In principio* with which the fourth gospel, like the book of *Genesis*, opens can be said to strike the keynote of the gospel. The Word is not the beginning but is in the beginning and in every true beginning; and wherever the Word is active, wherever the Light shines forth, there is a new beginning. And

in my end is my beginning:[1]

every death-in-Christ is baptismal, is a new birth; every Christ-shared darkness is a new dawn. The christian dark journey is not the unending, nostalgic, ineffectual circling of the mythological 'eternal return' but a progression in which each successive end achieved is a fulfilment but not a finality.

When the hour came for the Son to return to his Father, this end was a beginning: not the falling of the curtain when the drama is over, but the rising of the curtain on a new scene, the rending of the temple veil for the new approach to the newly accessible God. In the same way, when Mary's 'days were accomplished' and she brought forth her Son, this was a beginning; and when his childhood ended at Cana, this was a beginning, the 'beginning of miracles', the *initia* of the mysteries; and when on the cross he told her, 'Woman, that is your son', this was for her yet another beginning. And the death of Lazarus is a moment's sleep after which he comes forth from the tomb and begins a new day and attends a banquet; and perhaps in Christ's words to the Magdalen, 'Do not cling to me', we may read an injunction never to refuse a new beginning as long as the 'day's course', the time for working, lasts.

[1] This and the following quotations from Mr T. S. Eliot are from *East Coker* and *Little Gidding*.

For this is our temptation, to want to rest in achievement instead of surrendering it and going on to a new beginning. At noon the sun reaches its zenith, but it cannot linger there, it must go on, down into the darkness of renewal. At Sichar it was noon, and Christ was weary with journeying, but he spoke with urgency of the shortness of the working day, and of the fields golden and ripe for harvesting. It was noon when Pilate proclaimed, 'Here is the Man' and 'Here is your King', and brought the ineffable mystery of the mercy of the humiliated God to stand before the unspeakable squalor of the malice and misery of man; but this moment led on to the beginning of the *transitus*, Christ taking up his cross and carrying it to the dark place of the skull.

But from the dark place of the skull the tree rises till it touches and pierces the vault of heaven so that the rain and the snow can fall to bedew and renew the earth; and the last cry, *consummatum est*, 'the work is done', is the *initia*, the birth-announcement, *ecce nova facio omnia*, 'I make all things new' (*Apoc.* 21⁵): the Word makes 'a new heaven and a new earth' (*Apoc.* 21¹) because he achieves that *hierosgamos*, the 'sacred marriage' of heaven and earth, which is the culmination of the myth-hero's journey and which means the begetting of a new life, a new world.

We want to rest in achievement, to arrest the sun's course, even if our only achievement is acquiescence in failure, because as the day draws on we become wearied and haunted by what youth so easily ignores, the fear of the descent into darkness; we are weary and we want to

sit down not for a brief re-creative moment but indefi-
nitely, turning our backs on the well; surely we are too
old and tired to learn new tricks? But no:

old men ought to be explorers:

if we stopped seeing each dark-before-dawn as a new
beginning for us it would mean that the day of death was
dawning for us, the death of the soul; and even though
the new beginning may be a beginning of immobility, of
holding out our arms and letting another gird us and lead
us where we are not minded to go, still it is a new beginning of life for us; for every death in Christ and birth in
Christ is both mobile and immobile: the immobility of
the humble receptive *fiat*, and the mobility of readiness
for some new thing, even though the new thing may
seem to be merely the absence—or the stark, cruel
abstraction from us—of something old, and loved of old.

The readiness is all; and this readiness is faith: being
still, so as to hear and assimilate the word spoken to us,
and being mobile, so as to follow where we are led:

> *We must be still and still moving*
> *Into another intensity*
> *For a further union, a deeper communion*
> *Through the dark cold and the empty desolation,*
> *The wave cry, the wind cry, the vast waters . . .*

And faith is an affirmation, the readiness is a work spoken
in answer to the Word spoken. The Word is not the
beginning but is the source of all beginnings; and in each
new beginning there is the creative Word of God and the

responsive word of man. 'Do you truly *want* to be made whole?': the re-creative word is uttered if there is readiness to utter the responsive word. Living morality (as opposed to dead legalism) is dialogue: if the Word had not been uttered there could be no dialogue, if we had not been given to hear the divine word we could have had no word to utter in reply; we could have had an ethic of humanly conceived justice or righteousness, of human idealism, we could not have had the ethic according to which every good act consists essentially in saying 'I love you' to God.

Legalism is the death of law because it is the end of exploration; it is still but not still moving, and its stillness is not the dynamic stillness of readiness but the rigidity of a corpse. The legalists had 'shut [their] ears to the sound of his voice, had shut [their] eyes to any revealing of him' and so the living responsive word had become a lifeless legal document, neat, tidy, typed and taped and predictable, safely locked away from the swift, untidy, unpredictable Wind.

> *We shall not cease from exploration*
> *And the end of all our exploring*
> *Will be to arrive where we started*
> *And know the place for the first time:*

the gospel of the ministry begins with the words 'Follow me', and with those same words, spoken to Peter, the gospel ends; but between the two the journey has been made, and now the words have a new meaning and there can be a new beginning. The first beginning is in the turning of Jesus to ask 'What are you looking for?'; and for man there is a new beginning every time he turns anew to utter the reply of faith, every time he is converted afresh and can affirm a fresh readiness to follow.

Conversion, once again, is never pure passivity. If we pray, 'Turn us back to you and we shall be turned' we acknowledge the fact that to turn to God we must first receive from God the power to do so; but the receiving itself implies an activity, a positive willing; with us as with the mother of Jesus the offering of divine life requires an answering *fiat*; and then, when life and power have been received they must be used, we have to spring to new life out of the rigid immobility of death, as the cripple had to pick up his bed, the bed on which he had been immobilized, and walk.

But the quality of the outward activity must depend on the quality of the *fiat*, on the extent to which the self has been stripped and laid bare to the creative power; and always an essential part of that removal of obstacles is the destruction of activism with all its vanity and futility, stilling the superficial noise and bustle of our lives as Christ stilled the waves, killing our ego-reliance so as to become God-reliant and therefore in a true sense self-reliant, learning the truth of St Paul's assertion that while we can do nothing 'as of ourselves' we can do 'all things in him who strengthens' us. *Vacate et videte*: if we are to see the truth and hear the word we must first be still, our house must be at rest.

This is the other, the creative significance of sleep as a

symbol: that turning, with 'soul stilled, as a weaned child' (*Ps.* 130^2), to our own deepest sources and resources which is an essential moment in every creative and re-creative process. This is the sleep, not of inanition, but of germination, of prophetic ecstasy or of poetic inspiration, the moment described in the *Song of Songs*, 'I sleep, but my heart keeps watch' (5^2). In the beginning God 'cast a deep sleep upon Adam' (*Gen.* 2^{21}) before fashioning Eve; and Augustine points the parallel: 'Adam sleeps that Eve may be born; Christ dies that the Church may be born'. It was in sleep that Jacob saw the ladder, that the child Samuel heard the voice of the Lord, that Elijah was visited by the angel; in the gospel story it is while he is asleep that Joseph receives the angel's message. In humbler contexts there are plenty of parallels: we know how often problems which have baffled us seem to solve themselves when our busy and perhaps misguided ratiocinations are stilled, either when we are literally asleep— there is wisdom in the simple advice to 'sleep on it'—or during the metaphorical sleep which is abstention from conscious thought, a deliberate temporary shelving of the problem; similarly if we turn our attention away from a germinal idea or the first rough outline of a theme in music or art or rational discourse, we often find when we return to it that it has matured and taken shape, that what was muddled has now become clear. And this psychological rhythm of withdrawal, germination, and creative activity is found again in religious practice: in the periodical 'retreat' into quietude, away from the bustle of everyday life, in the daily withdrawal for a time into the quietude of prayer,[1] and in the attempt to achieve the stillness and tranquillity of 'recollection' in the midst of the lunatic clamour and frenzied tempo of life in the modern world.

The scriptures tell us that wisdom is 'more active than all active things' (*Wisd.* 7[24]); what looks like immobility may in fact be intense activity; the value of action, the depth of its influence and the lastingness of its effect, are measurable by the extent to which it springs from the stillness of contemplation. The power and authority of a truly great personality are recognized by the quietness with which they are exercised: there is no need to shout. In the Passion story our Lord is silent and unresisting, like the lamb before the shearers,[2] when they torture and humiliate him, but the silence expresses the certitude and plenitude of inner power, that power which Pilate sensed, and was filled with superstitious dread, so that he asked what manner of being Jesus was,[3] the power which caused those who came to arrest our Lord in the garden to shrink back and fall to the ground.[4]

[1] Unfortunately the essential quietude of prayer is often obscured nowadays by the activism which is so pervasive in religious practice: the false idea that in prayer the mind must be constantly, actively, 'busy about many things', and the superstitious belief that 'distractions', though quite unintentional (neither deliberately sought out nor, when adverted to, acquiesced in) and therefore inculpable, are sinful, so that the incessant activity must be redoubled in intensity to keep them at bay.

[2] cf. *supra*, p. 55.

[3] I have tried to convey this in the text by making Pilate's question a double one: 'What are you? Whence are you come?'

[4] We need not regard this event as miraculous in the sense of being quite outside the possibilities of natural psychic experience:

It was 'when all things were in quiet silence', we are told, that the 'almighty Word leapt down' from God's 'royal throne' (*Wisd.* 18[14, 15]) and became man; it was in the quiet silence of his own soul, while all external things were in tumult and clamour, that the Word came to the consummation of his earthly journey; and this inwardness is of immediate significance for ourselves: the christian journey is essentially an inner struggle and transformation, and we shall never be transfigured, never become apparelled in celestial light, if we try to escape the struggle by projecting or externalizing it, pretending that the darkness lies only outside us, in the *selva oscura*, the dark wood, of an external and alien world, not inside us, in our own blindness, our own pride and lusts and greeds.

But the Passion symbols throw further light on the idea of the christian journey as an imitation of the Christ-journey: each must make his own journey, carry his own cross, and every journey must follow the one essential pattern; but while the Light shows us the way, the Way (having pity on the multitudes) makes the way easy for us, the yoke gentle and the burden light; the cross which all but the very greatest of his followers are asked to bear

---

a somewhat similar incident is described by Mme David-Neel in her account of her travels in Tibet. What happens here is the effect, not of something Jesus *does* with 'extraordinary' power, but of the 'ordinary' (i.e. ever-present) power which *is* in his humanity by reason of his divinity: as Jerome says of the cleansing of the temple: 'A radiance and fire like that of the stars shone forth from his eyes, and his face revealed the majesty of Godhead' (*Comment. in Matth.* lib. iii, ad 21[15]).

is but a token-cross compared with his:[1] as the reality of
Golgotha is daily brought to us, truly and effectively but
in symbol, the shedding of blood replaced by the
'separating' of Body and Blood (and, as a secondary,
attendant parallel, the drinking of the vinegar, the *vin
aigre*, replaced by the drinking of the Wine), so in the
second sacrament, which gives strength and maturity,
the purely symbolic tap on the cheek replaces the slap of
the soldier's hand at the trial and the buffetings which
follow the crowning with thorns; and perhaps too, we may
see in the wand of the Roman penitentiary administering
the sacrament of repentance an infinitely distant echo of
the reality of the scourging.

Again and again the events of the Passion re-state in
dark and cruel form the symbols which originally por-
trayed the joy and innocence of paradise, but in so doing
they lead us onwards, and not only indicatively but
effectively, to the other paradise, the eternal life and joy
of heaven. John speaks not of Calvary but of Golgotha,
which means The Place of the Skull: that the name was
suggested by the shape of the hill is probable enough, but
according to an ancient tradition this was the place where
the skull of Adam was buried, and traditions which are

[1] The carrying of the cross to Golgotha corresponds—but also
stands in sharp contrast—to the episode of the *transitus* as it is often
found in the mythological night-journey. The myth-hero drags the
animal he has slain to a cave or the sea-shore and, having flayed it,
clothes himself in its skin so as to be indued with its strength; what
Christ carries is the instrument of the slaying since he is himself the
victim to be slain; and afterwards it is those who follow him and
have faith in him who are indued with the divine victim's life, who
'put on' Christ.

widespread and longstanding are, from the psychological point of view, to be treated with respect; moreover it is folly indeed to brush them aside as valueless fantasies by comparison with the solidly-based facts of history: the formation and development and survival of such traditions are themselves among the solid facts of history. The significance of the legend is obvious if we view it against the background of the twofold genesis, the creation and re-creation, of the world. The first Adam brings about the disintegration of mankind and of the world by trying to be a god instead of a man; the second Adam brings about the re-integration of mankind and of the world because, being both God and man, in him and by him (the ladder) the marriage of heaven and earth is achieved: heaven comes down to earth and therefore earthly life can be hallowed and made heavenly.

And as, in the imagery of *Genesis*, it is from the side of Adam that Eve is formed, and at his side that she stands as his helpmeet and the mother of men, so in *John* it is at the side of the crucified Christ that the second Eve stands, her com-passion the helpmeet to his Passion, and from that position at his side that her second vocation, the motherhood of men *in vitam aeternam*, is inaugurated. Thus, for mother as for Son, Calvary is the culmination of what was initiated at Cana: the 'beginning of the signs', the *initia* of the messianic *mystērion*, is also the moment of separation (itself proclaimed beforehand in the synoptic losing-and-finding story of the Child in the temple) when the Word must leave mother and home behind him and embark on his journey as a homeless

wanderer; and this is indicated by the title with which
Jesus addresses his mother. The vocative *gynai*, 'Woman',
implies no disrespect, still less any rebuke: it expresses a
formal courtesy; but for that very reason it is not a mode
of address commonly used by son to mother, and in the
Cana story it stands in sharp contrast to the immediately
preceding phrase, 'the mother of Jesus'; as Jesus, with
the performing of his first sign, passes from the status of
child[1] to that of Son of Man, so Mary is formally addressed
in terms of her vocation as second Eve, as Mother of Man,
a role which in 19[26] is as it were formally promulgated.
(Where *gynaï* is used elsewhere in the gospel I have
omitted it, partly for lack of a really adequate English

[1] It is possible to see a further reference to the ending of the
mother-child relationship in the words which follow, if we take
them as meaning 'Why do you trouble me with this?' (or, 'Leave
me alone') followed by 'My hour is not yet come'. The obvious
difficulty about any such reading is that Jesus does in fact proceed
at once to act on his mother's suggestion; and some modern scholars
have offered what seems a much more likely interpretation, reading
the last clause not as a statement but as a question, 'Has not my
hour come?' (The first clause can mean 'Leave it to me; don't
worry' as well as 'Leave me alone'.) The 'hour' of Jesus is the
moment of the manifesting of his glory; and this is essentially the
moment of his being 'lifted up' in crucifixion and ascension; but it
can also refer to his whole public life, or the initiation of it, as a
theophany of which the lifting up is the climax; and this latter
sense fits admirably here, since Cana is precisely the initiation of
the messianic work. Thus the ending of the mother-child relationship is much more forcibly indicated; and we can in consequence
allow the vocative its fullest implications, 'Woman' signifying 'the
second Eve', no longer simply 'the mother of Jesus' but now in
addition mother of all the race of men.

In the text which follows I have gratefully adopted this interpretation of the words of our Lord; and have translated: 'Woman,
why are you anxious? Has not my hour now come?'

equivalent, but also in order to bring into relief this special significance of 'Woman' in these two passages.)

The word *adam* means 'man': Adam *is* Man inasmuch as he is the origin of all humanity; Christ is Man, is The Man, inasmuch as he draws all men to himself (12^{32}) and all humanity, all creation, is summed up in him (*Ephes.* 1^9); through him the light of understanding is given to all men (*Jn.* 1^9) and through him humanity is given the new and eternal life which is in all those who are born anew from on high; more, he is Man because he is the Vine: through the divine interinanimation which he bestows on all who have faith in him, all are one with him and all are one in him; the tower of Babel, disintegrating the human family, is replaced by the tree of Golgotha, re-uniting the human family and integrating its human life in the life of God.

This glory too is achieved through the grim re-statement of the original paradisal themes: the new tree is the true tree both of life and of knowledge—the God-given life which is eternal, the God-given wisdom which comes through faith—but it is that because it is the rood-tree, the gibbet on Skull Hill. The re-statement brings about man's re-instatement, but it is by way of darkness; the tree is the tree of life-through-death, of knowledge-through-ignorance-accepted, the humble acceptance of the obscurity of faith.

Man is re-integrated in Christ because Christ is the Man of Sorrows. Once again glory is achieved through travesty. When Pilate told the crowd, 'Here is The Man', he knew not what he said; he had no idea of the perfect aptness of his words to proclaim the *Archanthrōpos*, the ideal or archetypal man; and what he said was said in mockery as he brought Jesus, wearing the crown of thorns, before the crowd; but he was in fact echoing the words of the Baptist, 'Here is the man who takes away the world's sin', the man who gave men back their humanity by giving them to share in his divinity.

This is one of the implications of the title by which our Lord often refers to himself, the Son of Man. The Son of Man is the ladder joining heaven and earth: he is both the one who descends from heaven and will later be seen in glory, the heavenly man, and the one who must suffer and die, the man of sorrows; he is the meeting-place of heaven and earth both in the soteriological sense, the mediator who brings about the at-one-ment of man with God, and in the ontological sense, the incarnate Word, truly God and truly man; he is also the *Archanthrōpos*, who being without sin and yet 'made sin for our sakes' can take away the world's sin and so bring about the transfiguring of mankind into his own image and likeness; he is thus both the efficient and the exemplary cause of our attainment of integrity, giving us the power to realize in ourselves the ideal man and showing us in his own flesh what that ideal is.

The Way makes the way easy for most of us; but having said this we may need to remind ourselves afresh that every man's journey must in essentials follow the pattern of Christ's, and that every man must make his own way: it cannot be made for him, and he may not rationalize his comfort-loving evasions of its asperities by regarding them as interventions of the divine pity, a divine accommodating of harsh reality to his weakness. In some way we must share in Christ's death if we are to share in his glory; in some degree we must like him be men of sorrows if we are to have his joy in us, filling our hearts brimful.

And since the journey means being transformed from disintegration into integrity it must involve facing, accepting, redeeming and so integrating the darkness that is in us, our own dark shadow. Moses lifts up the serpent in the desert that the people may gaze upon it: they must face their own evil in order to be cured: if they refuse to face it they are incurable because they are wilfully blind. And to gaze with faith at the Word on the tree is to see in his unblemished light the measure of our own darkness and therefore of our need of being made whole.

10. Integration and Glory

Symbol clarifies for us the nature of the individual's inner conflicts by externalizing them, turning them into struggles between two antagonists. In the same sort of way John, with his sense of drama, uses the device of dialogue to clarify doctrine—a dialogue which starts from initial incomprehension on the one side so as to elicit elucidations from the other. And as the history of Esau and Jacob for example can profitably be studied as an externalization of Jacob's own personal search for integrity, so perhaps it is permissible to consider some of the secondary characters in *John* as representing, in relation to our Lord, the dark shadow which is in all of us, waiting (and perhaps clamouring) for redemption and integration.

It is particularly tempting to make this identification in the case of the apostle whose name, Thomas or Didymus, means 'the twin'. He is much more prominent in John than in the synoptics; his misunderstandings (11^{16}; 14^5) and his refusal to believe (20^{24-9}) are functionally important; almost every time he is mentioned his name is translated as though to remind us that he is a twin yet we are never told anything of the other twin, and in early times a theory was formed according to which he was the twin of our Lord himself, and he was identified with the Judas who is one of the four 'brethren' (the hebraism meaning 'cousins') of Jesus mentioned in the synoptics; thus the *Gospel according to Thomas* describes the *logia* or sayings which it contains as 'the secret words which the living Jesus spoke and Didymos Judas Thomas wrote'.

The world of symbol contains many examples of twins or other pairs (brothers, friends) who stand in contrast to one another and represent the different sides of or elements in the human personality. Every man has his 'dark' side; but 'dark' must not be taken in this context as synonymous with 'evil', for the dark side comprises all the qualities which have been consciously or unconsciously rejected by the *persona* and all those which have never emerged into the light of day at all but remain

hidden as undeveloped potentialities. The contrast between the brothers may be presented as between mortal
and immortal, or carnal man and spiritual man, or again
natural and ideal man: the inner psychological fact thus
represented is our need of transformation into the 'other
being' within us, the greater personality we ought to be;
and this greater personality is, in christian terms, the
likeness of the Son of Man, the *Archanthrōpos*, into
which it is the purpose of the dark journey to transform
us. The old Adam in us must be transfigured into the
likeness of the new; and this means a change of mind and
heart alike: a change-over from egocentricity to theo-
centricity, from selfishness to love, from blindness to
wisdom, from life-rejection to life-acceptance, from the
proud folly of attempted autonomy to the humble docility
and freedom of faith.

Thomas, though loyal and eager to follow where Christ
may lead, lacks understanding (when he speaks of meeting death with Christ he speaks truly, but it is a truth he
has not rightly grasped); and he lacks faith, refusing to
accept what he cannot see and feel for himself, till, confronted by the Truth, he is transfigured; then, his final
words express a total acceptance of Christ and of himself
in Christ, of his true self, his creaturely stature but also
his identification with Christ as a branch of the Vine; and
his 'My Lord and my God' contains by implication the
mystic's assertion, 'My Me is God'.

There is a similar lesson to be learnt from the encounter
between Mary Magdalen and the risen Christ. Scholars
disagree as to the meaning of Christ's words to her, and

one must choose which theory to follow; I have adopted the suggestion that Christ tells her she must not cling to him because he has not yet ascended to the Father, meaning that the time for the sabbath rest and joy of heaven, the *interminabilis vitae tota simul et perfecta possessio*,[1] is not yet come for her, there is still work to be done demanding generosity and self-sacrifice. Of the greatness of Mary's love there is no question; but if this reading is correct we must assume that it was not yet fully perfected in selflessness: 'Do not cling to me' means in effect 'Do not be greedy or impatient; make your heart ready to wait for the joy of heaven till the work of the earthly journey is done'. For heaven comes only when egocentricity is completely abolished.

Mary had to acquire the strength to be perfect in patience; Peter, impulsive and inclined to be over-sanguine, had to acquire patience enough to be strong. His transfiguration is manifested in the thrice-asked question 'Do you love me?', which matches and abolishes his triple denial; at the third asking he was 'distressed', but not impatient: he was ready now to be told 'When you are grown old you will hold out your arms to let another tie your belt about you and lead you where you are not minded to go': he was strong enough to be shown what these words meant, the 'kind of death by which he was to glorify God' (21^{15-19}).

Thus in these three, in their different ways and in accordance with their different needs, wholeness is

[1] 'The total and simultaneous possession of unending life' (Boethius: *De Consol. Philos.* v. 6).

achieved through the perfecting in them of the image of the Son of Man, sublime and humble, wholly dedicated to God. Those to whom great power and authority are entrusted stand especially in need of these qualities if they are to use their power creatively and not destructively both for others and for themselves. This is perhaps the explanation of the fact that when the risen Christ breathes on the disciples and gives them the power of the Spirit to heal and hallow the souls of men, the still doubting Thomas is not with them. This scene is not to be confused with the coming of the Spirit at Pentecost (though the circumstances of the one—the little assembly, *ecclesia*, of apostles, the locked doors, the breath of life— suggest the other): the essential meaning of the pentecostal wind and fire is the transfiguring of the apostles themselves into complete affinity with the Fire; here in this earlier scene the emphasis is all the time on power: our Lord's own power manifested in the passing through the locked door, and the bestowal of power through the breathing into them, the inspiring, of his own life-breath: they are empowered now to begin the building of the Church; after Pentecost they will *be* the Church, for Pentecost is the divine establishment of the Church and they are its foundation-stones.

One of John's most striking characteristics is his ability to combine sublimity with homeliness. His gospel opens with the immensities of the Godhead, the portrayal of the eternal Word; and when he goes on to speak of the incarnate Word and to unfold the story of his earthly journey, that background of immensity is always present, we are never allowed to lose sight of the infinity of life and power and majesty hidden in and revealed through the human flesh; yet at the same time he constantly emphasizes the humanness of the Word and the humble, homely, human realities of the life he lived amongst us: the Word knows hunger and thirst; is tired by his journey and must sit down by the well; is sad and troubled and weeps; is so filled with distress and anger that he groans aloud; he loves friendship and fellowship, he feasts with his friends and his friends know they can count on his help; he has his beloved disciple, who leans on him at the supper. And the gospel ends with an episode (the last chapter) in which this combination of homely and sublime is particularly striking.

This final chapter is an appendix added either by John or by a disciple—which explains why the gospel as we know it has two conclusions, 20^{30-1} and 21^{25}; the obvious thing, if we are to incorporate this chapter into the gospel, seems to be to make one single conclusion out of these two texts, and this I have done.

Fittingly the chapter assembles many of the universal rebirth-symbols: the sea, the boat, the seven men, the long and arduous night-labours; then the dawn, the catch of fish, the naked Peter, the fire, the bread. And, as in the story of Mary Magdalen in the resurrection-garden, though it is dawn the light is not yet good; we are still in the obscurity of faith; only great love can discern the identity of the figure on the sea-shore: the beloved disciple tells Peter, 'It is the Lord'. It is the Lord risen and glorious, and he will speak of what the great catch of fish symbolizes, the Church's universal apostolate; he will speak of feeding his sheep and leading them to pasture; finally he will speak of death, of martyrdom, he will bid Peter follow him *usque ad mortem*, even to the death of the cross—his description of Peter holding out his arms and letting another gird him is a clear reference to crucifixion. But on the other hand he shouts to them across the water in simple, almost racy language;[1] it is he (we are to suppose) who makes a fire and cooks a meal on it; and then, calling to them to come and eat, he serves the food to each of them. And all this mingling of divine and human, of sublimity and homeliness, of solemnity and gaiety, is summed up brilliantly, startlingly, in the statement of the size of the catch: a hundred and fifty-three fishes.

On the one hand this number is a dramatically emphasized symbol of totality or completeness. According to ancient Greek zoology there were 153 different kinds of fish in the sea. But the number itself is a 'triangular number': being the sum of the numbers 1 to 17 it can be set out as an equilateral triangle comprising 153 dots, with 17 dots to each side; moreover 17 is made up of 7 and 10, each of which taken by itself is a symbol of completeness. The catch of fish therefore is perfect, total and universal: we are in the presence of the immensity of God's all-embracing love. But, on the other hand, what of the literal sense: how can so odd a number be part of

[1] There is really no way of conveying in English the full flavour of the word our Lord uses to address them (*paidia, filioli*, lit. 'little children'), with its mixture of cheerful informality, friendliness, humour and tenderness, except by resorting to slang.

the story? There is surely only one answer, and it is a very simple one: the disciples, the *paidia*, were so excited by the size of the catch, coming on top of their night-long failure,[1] that they had to know at once just how big it was.

So the gospel ends with the perfect meeting and marriage of heaven and earth, the theandric quality of the new life, the holiness of reborn humanity, the humanness of christian holiness. Pious people are apt to be rather inhuman; holy people never. The Word did not become man in order to rob man of his humanity but to perfect it, to make what is humanly lovely divinely lovely as well. Evelyn Underhill pointed out how the saints 'enjoy the high spirits peculiar to high spirituality: and shock the world by a delicate playfulness, instead of exhibiting the morose resignation which it feels to be proper to the "spiritual life". . . . Dante, initiated into Paradise, sees the whole universe laugh with delight as it glorifies God'.[2]

Sublimity is simplicity. Nothing in the gospel leads us to suppose that to be holy is an easy matter; everything leads us to suppose that it is a simple one. As all the muddled superstitions of legalism are swept away by the one command of love and by the lovely mystery of interinanimation, so all the superstitious frenzies of the pietistic activist, all the false and destructive asceticisms which are in all the various forms of manicheism, all the portrayals of heaven as wholly unrelated to the values of earth, and of holiness as identical with inhumanity: all are swept

---

[1] 'Apart from me you can do nothing' (15[5]).
[2] *Mysticism*, p. 438.

away by the profound simplicity of this lovely final scene, in which the might and majesty of the Word are manifested in the homeliness of human love and fellowship, the humble breaking of bread together, and the fish cooking on the fire.

NOTE ON THE TEXT

NOTE ON THE TEXT

a. Structure of the Gospel

The body of the gospel, from the end of the prologue onwards, falls naturally into three main sections:

1. 1^{19} to the end of 12: the public ministry,
2. 13 to 17 inclusive: Jesus alone with the twelve,
3. 18 to the end: Passion and Glory.

It is convenient, however, to subdivide the first of these sections; and here, while some parts stand out clearly as units (the sixth chapter for instance, concerned with the Bread of Life), opinions differ as to the best method of division. For the purposes of this present study it seemed best to avoid too lengthy sections; and I have therefore divided the first main section into seven parts, and the second section into two, thus:

	1^{1-18}:	Prologue
1.	$1^{19}-2^{11}$:	The New Order Opens
2.	$2^{12}-4^{46}$:	The Living Water
3.	$4^{46}-5^{47}$:	The Living Word
4.	6:	The Living Bread
5.	7 and 8:	Plottings of the Blind
6.	9 and 10:	Light and Shepherd of the World
7.	11 and 12:	Death and Life in Duel

8. 13^{1-30}:   The Last Supper
9. $13^{31}-17^{26}$: The Last Discourse
10. 18–end: Passion and Glory

The beginning of each chapter of the traditional division of the text has been printed in the margin; the two main textual transpositions (of 7^{19b-24} and 8^{1-11}) are pointed out in footnotes in the text; the other, minor, transpositions are not marked in the text but are noted here, in the following section.

b. Textual Transpositions

The purpose of these changes is the purely practical one of trying to make the sense of the text, and especially of our Lord's discourses, easier to follow.

In the Prologue, ll. 4–10 of the present text are an expansion of 1^2; and 1^9 has been joined on to 1^3 to make ll. 11–16. 1^{15} has been omitted so as not to break the sequence of thought, since the content of the verse appears immediately below in $1^{19, \ 30}$; and 1^{18} has been inserted in its place, before 1^{16}.

There is a marked contrast in this gospel between those occasions when the mention of time and place is of great significance (noon, night, garden, etc.) and other occasions when such details seem to have no special significance and might indeed seem to have been added by some other hand than John's. 1^{28} and the last part of 1^{39} are cases in point; and I have incorporated these in 1^{19} and 1^{35} respectively in the hope of thus avoiding any slowing down of the tempo of the narrative.

The Jerusalem Bible[1] states, as a fact needing no argument, that 7^{19b-24} is displaced and should follow on 5^{16}: this change certainly seems of practical utility and I have therefore made it. Again there seems to be no doubt that the story of the adulteress (8^{2-11}) is not part of the original text of John; the only question is where to place it, since as it stands it interrupts the thread of our Lord's thought while, as explained above, it seems to be too important, and to fit too organically into the body of the gospel, to be relegated to an appendix; I have therefore put it at the end of the chapter, so that it leads straight on to the sign of the blind man, and have combined 8^1 with 8^{59}.

The difficulty presented by the last sentence of 14^{31} is well known: if they left the supper-room at this point how can it be said that they 'went out' in 18^1? For practical purposes the difficulty is solved by incorporating the former sentence into the latter; and this I have done. The equally obvious difficulty presented by 18^{15-23}—that these events took place at the house of Caiphas not, as the text suggests, of Annas—is solved by putting 18^{24} immediately after 18^{14}.

Finally there is the question of the last chapter and of the two endings to the gospel, 20^{30-1}, 21^{25}. For this study only one solution seemed conceivable, and I have adopted it: regarding 21 as indeed the last chapter of the gospel, and incorporating 20^{30-1} into 21^{25}.

---

[1] The French translation issued by the *Ecole Biblique de Jérusalem* under the direction of Père de Vaux, O.P.

c. *Adaptations of the Text*

It should perhaps be emphasized again that the text which follows is not a translation but an adaptation of the text of the gospel. The question must however be asked whether any such adaptation is not to be regarded as an irreverent and inexcusable tampering. (One thinks of Gounod's efforts with the first of the 48 Preludes.) But the answer is surely clear enough. Suppose for instance you want to tell children the story about the publican in the temple: you know that 'pharisee' is a difficult term for them, and 'publican' positively misleading; so you say 'Once upon a time two men went into church to say a prayer; one of them was highly respected, a pillar of the parish, but the other was looked down on because he was thought to be crooked in his ways of making money' etc.: quite certainly you are neither being irreverent, because you would not bother to make the original story clear unless you valued and reverenced it, nor tampering with the text or trying to improve on it, because your purpose is precisely to make the text accessible to the children's minds. And we do not outgrow the need for elucidation and re-presentation merely by growing up in years.

In the present case, however, there is a particular practical difficulty arising from the fact that the text given here does on the whole keep closely to the original, and therefore unless a reader is very familiar with the gospel he may find it difficult to distinguish original text from additional words or phrases put in to elucidate it. One's first intention was to find some typographical means of marking all additions to the original text; but one soon discovered that this could be done only at the cost of making the book unreadable and thus defeating its whole purpose. And even if one did decide, say, to print all additions in italics or enclosed in square brackets, despite the ugliness of these devices, still there would remain the difficulty of deciding exactly what constituted an addition. To say for instance in 11[33] that Christ groaned with grief and anger is not to add anything to the words of John, since the concept of anger is contained in the Greek verb; to say that Pilate shrugged as he asked 'What is truth?' (18[38]) is certainly to add to the text, though one can argue that the addition is implicit in the context; while to substitute praying 'as my children' for praying 'in my name' is not to add to the text but to interpret it— and as for interpretations, how is one to differentiate (other than by endless footnote references) between the generally accepted, the widely accepted, and the minority opinions?

In view of all these difficulties I decided in the end that I must let my own text stand as it is in the hope that it will be read simply for what it is: an individual and tentative 'portrayal' of, and introduction to, the thought of St John and the content of his gospel.

There are many places in the gospel where the exact meaning is debatable, either because of variations in the different Greek MSS, or because of differences between many of these and the Latin of the Vulgate, or, finally, because of some ambiguity or other obscurity inherent in the wording of a universally accepted text. (Some of the more important of these have been noted in the foregoing pages.) The practical question to be settled with regard to these passages is whether to try to give all the various interpretations in each case or to decide on one and ignore the rest: the latter method is obviously the less scholarly but is the more simple, avoiding the heavy array of footnotes which the former would entail, and therefore I have chosen it. I should add that I have been guided throughout the gospel mainly by the text and notes of the Jerusalem Bible and the commentary of Lagrange, but also by other standard works, catholic and non-catholic, on the gospel and especially on the philology of the text; so far as the choice of vocabulary in my own text is concerned I have consulted, and plundered, all available English versions, traditional and modern-colloquial, and have tried to make my own decisions as to what might best convey the Greek by also referring constantly to the French versions and the various studies just mentioned. Unfortunately it is impossible to make adequate particular acknowledgements of one's debts: one tries to grasp the exact meaning of a word or phrase in the original, then one studies the various different renderings of it, then broods, experiments, makes decisions only to alter or discard and start again, till in the end it is almost always impossible to say where the final version has come from. I know, for instance, that I owe the choice of 'flogging' and 'jeering' in place of 'scourging' and 'mocking' to Dr C. S. Lewis's *Introduction* to the Phillips translation of the epistles; on the other hand there are words and phrases which I am sure are my own; but then there are the many uncertainties: having for instance invented (as I thought) 'How long are you going to keep us on tenterhooks?' for 10^{24} I then noticed that the Rieu translation, which I had presumably seen beforehand, was substantially the same, so that the supposed invention was very probably an unconscious appropriation. My debts must therefore be acknowledged *in globo*: I can only say that where readers think they discern any given derivation they are probably right. I must also express my deep gratitude to friends on both sides of the Atlantic for their help, as patient and painstaking as it was valuable: to the biblical scholars among them for rescuing me from many a morass of perplexities and dubieties, and to them and others also for rescuing me from stylistic infelicities of one sort or another and for many valuable suggestions.

I am very conscious of the fact that, just as the foregoing *Introduction* merely touches on a few of the inexhaustible themes of the gospel, so the text which follows leaves many a problem unsolved, and solves (or side-tracks) others in ways which will doubtless fail to find favour with many a reader. But my task was attempted, not in the impossible hope of pleasing all readers but in the more modest hope of helping some: and of helping precisely by encouraging them to go on to a deeper study and therefore a deeper understanding of the 'real thing', the word of the eagle himself, and so of that vision of the Word which the eagle reveals to us.

THE
EAGLE'S WORD

The Prologue

1   In the beginning was the Word[1]
   and the Word was with God
   and the Word was God.
For the Word of God,
  the Wisdom of God,[2]
   is the Son of God:
and before the world was made
          and time began
  always God lived
and the Son was with the Father.[3]

It was through the Word
  that all things were made:
through him life is given
  to all that is,
through him the light of understanding
  is given to all men.
For his life is light:[4]
  a light shining out in the darkness.
And the darkness cannot master it.

A man was sent by God—
  John was his name—

[1] cf. pp. 13, 42–5.   [2] cf. pp. 16–17.
[3] cf. p. 17n.   [4] cf. pp. 13–14, 21 *sqq.*

to proclaim the coming of the Light[1]
  and bear witness to the Light
    that all men might believe in the Light.
He was not the Light:
  he was to bear witness to the Light.
The true[2] Light, the Word,
  who gives light to all men
    came down into the world.
The Light came
  and shone out in the darkness of the world.[3]
The Word became man
  and lived among men in the world.
But the world would not welcome the Word,
  the darkness would not receive the Light;
    the Son came to his own people
but his own people turned him away.
Yet some there were who did believe in him
                and welcome him:
  to these he gave a new life,
          God's life,
  gave them power to become God's children—
by a birth springing not from human seed
          nor the hunger of the flesh
          nor the will of a man
             but from God—
  that as he lived among men
    so they might live always with God.

The Word became human flesh and blood[4]

[1] cf. p. 35.   [2] cf. p. 46.   [3] cf. pp. 38–9.   [4] cf. p. 68n.

and lived[1] for a time amongst us:
and so, with our own eyes,
　we saw the Lord's Glory,[2]
　the glory which is his alone,
　　God's Son,
　　gracious and true.
For no man has ever seen God;
　but now his Son,
　　living always with the Father,
　has shown us clearly what God is.
And he has given us all to share
　in the fullness of his life,
a new life for us in place of the old:
　no longer simply the law
　　as given to man by Moses,
　but life, gracious and true,
　　brought to man by Christ.

1. *The New Order Opens*

And John bore witness,
　he proclaimed the truth:
while he was baptizing at Bethany
　　　　　beyond the Jordan
the pharisees sent priests and levites
　from Jerusalem to ask him, Who are you?
and he replied at once,

[1] cf. pp. 14–15.　[2] cf. pp. 13–15, 21, 86.

I am not the Christ.[1]

They asked,

    Are you then Elijah?

and again he said,

    I am not.

    Are you Moses, the great prophet?

and he answered, No.

They said:

    Tell us then who you are;

      give an account of yourself

        that we may account to those who sent us.

John told them:

    I am what the prophet Isaiah spoke of:

    a voice,

      crying in the wilderness:

        Make ready for the Lord's coming.

Then they asked him:

    But why do you baptize

      if you are not the Christ

                nor Elijah

                nor the great prophet?

He answered:

    I baptize only with water.

    But there is one in your midst

      whom you do not know:

        he, though he comes after me,

---

[1] The literal meaning of *Christos* (Gk) and *Messiah* (Hebr.) is 'anointed', i.e. one anointed and consecrated by God for some saving mission. David, for example, is thus referred to in the psalms; but the title is applied pre-eminently to the 'true' David, 'the one who is to come', the Saviour.

   must yet take rank before me:
I am not worthy to untie the strap of his shoe.

Next day, John saw Jesus coming towards him, and he
cried out:
   Here is the Lamb of God,[1]
   here is the man who takes away the world's sin,[2]
   here is the man of whom I said
      that one would come after me
         who would yet take rank before me:
            for before I began to be,
               already he lived.
   I too did not know him for what he is,
      though it was to make him known to Israel
         that I was sent to baptize.
   I did not know him
      till I saw the Spirit[3] coming
         like a dove from heaven
            and resting upon him.
   Then I did know.
   For then I remembered
      what he who sent me to baptize with water
         told me:
            The one on whom you shall see
            the Spirit come down and rest,
   he it is who shall baptize with the holy Spirit.
   And now I have seen.
      Now I know.

   [1] cf. pp. 55 *sqq.*, 97 *sqq.*   [2] cf. p. 111.   [3] cf. p. 21.

And now I declare to you:
this is the Son of God.

Again on the following day, about four in the afternoon,
John was standing with two of his disciples when Jesus
walked by them. John, gazing upon him, cried:
There is the Lamb of God.
The two disciples, hearing him say this, followed Jesus.
Jesus turned,
saw them following him,
and asked them:
What are you looking for?[1]
They said to him:
Master, where is your dwelling-place?
He answered:
Come and see.
So they went,
and saw the place where he was staying;
and they remained with him
all the rest of that day.

Now one of these two, who heard what John said and
followed Jesus, was Andrew the brother of Simon Peter.
He, at daybreak, went in search of Simon his brother and
told him: We have found the Christ. And he brought him
to Jesus.
Jesus, gazing upon him, said:
You are Simon son of Jonah:

[1] cf. pp. 44–5.

one day you shall be called Peter, the Rock.

Next day, Jesus decided to set out for Galilee. He met
Philip, who was from Bethsaida where Andrew and Peter
also lived; and he said to him:

Follow me.

Philip found Nathanael, and told him:

We have found him of whom Moses and the prophets
spoke:

it is Jesus son of Joseph, from Nazareth.

Nathanael said:

Nazareth?

Can anything good come from Nazareth?

Philip answered:

Come and see.

When Jesus saw Nathanael coming towards him he said:

Here is a true son of Israel, a man without guile.

Nathanael asked him:

How is it you know me?

Jesus answered:

When you were under the fig-tree,[1]

before Philip called to you,

I saw you.

Nathanael said:

Master, you are the Son of God, the king of Israel.

But Jesus replied:

You believe because I said I saw you under the fig-tree?

Truly, you shall see greater things than that.

I tell you, you shall all see the heavens opened

[1] cf. p. 53n[2].

and the angels of God going up and coming down
upon the Son of Man.[1]

2   On the third day after this there was a wedding feast at
Cana in Galilee.[2] The mother of Jesus was there; and
Jesus and his disciples were also among the guests. During
the feast the wine gave out; and the mother of Jesus said
to him:

They have no wine.

He answered:

Woman, why are you anxious?

Has not my hour now come?[3]

Then she said to the wine-servers:

Whatever he tells you to do, do it.

There were six large water-jars of stone standing there,
for the ritual washings customary among the Jews.[4]
Jesus said to the servers:

Fill the jars with water.

They filled them, brimful.

Then he told them:

Draw now

and serve the master of the feast.

They did so.

And the master of the feast tasted the water which had
now been turned into wine. Then, not knowing where it
came from, for only the servers knew that, he called to
the bridegroom and said to him:

Always the best wine is set out first,

[1] cf. p. 49.   [2] cf. pp. 58–9, 108–9   [3] cf. p. 109n.   [4] cf. pp. 58–9.

and then, when men have drunk deep and are merry,[1]
  the poorer kind:
but you have kept the best wine until now.

So, at Cana in Galilee, Jesus did this, his first sign,[2]
  and made known his glory,
    and his disciples believed in him.

2. *The Living Water*

After this he went down to Capharnaum with his mother
and relatives and disciples, and they stayed there for a few
days. Then, as the Jewish feast of the pasch was drawing
near, Jesus went up to Jerusalem. And in the temple he
found men selling oxen and sheep and doves, and money-
changers sitting at their desks. So he made a whip out of
cords and drove them all, men and sheep and oxen, out
of the temple. He overturned the desks of the money-
changers, scattering all their coins. And to the dove-
sellers he said:

  Take these away;
    and never again make my Father's house
      a market-place.[3]
His disciples then recalled the words of the scriptures:
  I am consumed with zeal for the honour of your house.
But the Jews[4] said to him:
  What sign can you give us
    to justify your doing this?

[1] cf. p. 59.   [2] cf. pp. 30–2.   [3] cf. pp. 20, 60.   [4] cf. p. 69n.

Jesus answered:
    Destroy this temple
    and in three days I will raise it up again.
The Jews cried:
    This temple took forty-six years to build,
      and you will raise it up again in three days?
But the temple Jesus spoke of was his body.
And later, when he had risen from the dead,
   his disciples recalled this saying,
     and so were made firm in believing
       both the scriptures which proclaim him
       and the words of him whom the scriptures proclaim.

There were many who did come to believe in him while
he was in Jerusalem for the feast, because of the signs
which he showed to them.
But he put no trust in them:
   he knew their kind;
nor did he need to be told about them by anyone:
   he knew what was in their hearts;
for he knew all men
   and all that is in the hearts of men.

3   Among the pharisees there was a man named Nicodemus,
one of the rulers of the Jews. This man came by night to
see Jesus, and said to him:
   Master, we know you are come from God to teach us,
    for no one could do the signs you do
     if God were not with him.

Jesus answered:

I tell you truly:

unless a man be born anew, from on high,

he can never see God's kingdom,

never have in him the life which is eternal.[1]

Nicodemus said:

But how can a man be born when he has once grown
old?

Can he go back into his mother's womb

and so be born anew?

Jesus answered him:

I tell you truly:

unless a man be born of water and the holy Spirit

he cannot enter God's kingdom.

What is born of mortal flesh is itself but mortal flesh;

what is born of the Spirit is itself spirit.

Do not wonder then that I tell you

you must be born anew, from on high.

Think how the wind blows where it will:

you hear its breath

but you cannot know the way it comes to you,

the way it goes from you:

so it is with all who are born

of the breath of the Spirit.[2]

Nicodemus said again:

But how can these things come about?

Jesus answered:

You do not understand,

[1] cf. p. 18. [2] cf. p. 21.

you, a master in Israel?[1]
I tell you truly:
  we speak of what we know,
  we declare what we have seen with our eyes,
    and yet you will not accept what we say.
If you do not trust me
  when I speak to you of earthly things,
how will you trust me
  when I tell you of heavenly things?
No man has ever gone up into heaven;
  but there is one who has come down from heaven:
  the Son of Man, whose home is heaven.
And as the serpent was lifted up
  by Moses in the wilderness,[2]
so must the Son of Man be lifted up,
  that all who, gazing upon him,[3] have faith in him[4]
  may have within them the life which is eternal.
For God so loved the world
  that he gave up to death
  his only Son
that all who have faith in him
  should not perish
    but should have life eternal.
It was for this that God
  sent him into the world:

---

[1] lit. 'the master': to appreciate the delicate irony of our Lord's words one should think of some such equivalent as 'And yet it's you who are the Doctor of Divinity, not I'.

[2] cf. pp. 27, 33.   [3] cf. pp. 27–8, 33, 46.

[4] cf. pp. 25–6, 41–5, 70.

not to condemn the world
  but to save the world.[1]
No man shall be condemned
  who gives his faith to the Son.
But those who refuse their faith
  are condemned already:
  when they refuse they condemn themselves.
  When the light came into the world
    some men fled the light:
  they preferred their darkness
    because of their evil deeds;
  for whoever does evil hates the light
              and flees from it
  lest the evil he does be discovered.
But he whose life is gracious and true,
  he comes into the light
    that what he does may be seen
      as done in God.

After this, Jesus went with his disciples into the country-side of Judaea, and remained with them there, baptizing. John also was baptizing (he had not yet been thrown into prison) at a place called Aenon or The Springs, near Salim, where there was plenty of water; and many went to him to be baptized. But a dispute arose between John's disciples and a man of Judaea about the value of ritual cleansings;[2] and they went to John and said to him:

[1] cf. pp. 71, 81–2.

[2] The man presumably drew an unfavourable contrast between John's baptism and that of Christ, and so provoked John's disciples into complaining to him of the people's defection.

Master, the man who was with you across the Jordan,
  and to whom you bore witness,
   is now baptizing
  and all the people are flocking to him.
John answered:
  A man can lay claim to nothing
   but what has been given him from heaven.
  You yourselves heard me say:
   I am not the Christ,
   I was sent before him to prepare the way.
  Only the bridegroom has the bride;
   yet the bridegroom's friend
    who stands close by him, listening,
     rejoices to hear the bridegroom's voice:
   and that joy is now mine, in full measure.
  He must count more and more;
   I, less and less.
  He who comes from above
   is above all men.
  He who comes from the earth
   is himself earthly
    and must speak the language of earth.
  He who comes from heaven
   speaks the words of God,
    given him in full measure
    by the Spirit of God:
he speaks of what he has seen and heard.
The world will not accept his words;
  but those who do accept them
   acknowledge and declare in so doing

that the words of God are true.
For the Father loves his Son
 and so has given all things into his hands.
He then who believes in the Son
 has within him the life which is eternal;
he who refuses to believe
 will never see that life:
  it is God's wrath that lives within him.

Jesus now learned that the pharisees had been told he was making more disciples and baptizing greater numbers than John (though it was not Jesus himself but his disciples who were baptizing). So he left Judaea and set out again for Galilee. This meant he would pass through Samaria. And on his way he came to a city called Sichar, near the land given by Jacob to his son Joseph, where there is a well called Jacob's Well.[1] Here Jesus sat down, by the well, for he was weary after his journey.
It was about noon.[2]
Presently a Samaritan woman came to draw water from the well. Jesus asked her to give him some that he might drink. (His disciples had gone into the city to buy food.) The woman said to him:

How is it that you, a Jew,
 ask water to drink from me, a Samaritan?
For the Jews will have nothing to do with the Samaritans.
Jesus answered:
 If you only knew the gift God offers
  and who I am who asked you for water,

[1] cf. pp. 55, 62.　[2] cf. pp. 62, 100.

you would have been asking me for water
and I would have given you the gift,[1]
the gift of living water.
The woman said to him:
But, sir, you have nothing with which to draw it out,
and the well is deep:
how could you have living water to give me?[2]
Are you greater than our father Jacob
who gave us this well
and drank of its waters
as did his sons also and his cattle?
Jesus answered:
Any man who drinks of this water
will after a time be thirsty again.
But the man who drinks of the water I give him
will never know thirst again;
for the water I give him
will become a living spring within him,
bearing him into the life which is eternal.
The woman cried:
Sir, give me then of this water
that I may never know thirst again
or need again to come here to draw water.
Jesus told her:
Go and fetch your husband
and then come back.
She replied:
I have no husband.
Jesus said:

[1] cf. pp. 62–3.   [2] cf. p. 62.

You are right: you have no husband.
You have had five,
  and the man you live with now is not your husband:[1]
  that indeed is true.
The woman answered:
  Sir, I see you are a prophet.
  Tell me then:
    our fathers of old worshipped on this mountain;
    how then can you hold
    that all should worship in Jerusalem?
Jesus said:
  Believe me, the hour is coming
    when you will go neither to this mountain
                  nor to Jerusalem
    to worship the Father.
  You do not know what you worship;
   we do know what we worship,
   for it is from the Jewish people
    that the saving of the world will come.
  Nevertheless the hour is coming,
   is indeed already come,
    when all true worshippers
     will offer to the Father
      that worship which is real and life-giving:[2]
   these are the worshippers the Father would have.
  For God is life-giving Spirit;
   therefore the worship given him
    must be real and life-giving.
The woman said:

[1] cf. p. 90. [2] cf. p. 63.

I know that the Messiah (that is, the Christ)
  is to come,
and when he comes
  he will make all these things clear to us.
Jesus answered:
  He is speaking to you:
      I AM he.

The disciples now returned. They were astonished to find
him talking with a woman,[1] yet none of them asked him
what he was questioning her about or why he was talking
with her.
The woman, leaving her water-pot, ran back to the city
and cried out to the people there: Come with me: I will
show you a man who has told me the whole story of my
life: must not this be the Christ?
So they left the city and went back with her to see him.
Meanwhile the disciples were urging him to eat. But he
told them:
  I have food to eat which you do not know of.
They asked one another:
  Can someone have brought him food?
Jesus said to them:
  My food is to do the will of him who sent me,
    to carry out to the end the task he set me.
  Is there not a saying common among you,
    'Twixt sowing and reaping
    four months must run?
  But of my harvest this is not so.

[1] cf. p. 89.

I tell you,
  lift up your eyes,
  look at the fields around you:
    already they are golden,
      ripe for the harvesting;
    already the reaper is receiving his wage,
      gathering in his master's crop
        for the life eternal
    where sower and reaper rejoice together.
  But there is another saying:
  One man sows,
  another reaps the fruit of his toil.
  And in this the saying is true:
  I send you out to reap what you have not sown.
    Others have toiled;
      you inherit the fruit of their toil.

Now many of the Samaritans of that city, when they
heard how Jesus had told the woman the story of her life,
were led to believe in him. So, when they came out to
him, they begged him to stay with them. And he did stay
with them for two days. As a result, many more believed
because of what he himself said to them. They told the
woman: We do not believe now because of your account
of him. We have heard him for ourselves. Now we know
he is indeed the Saviour of the world.

When the two days had gone by, Jesus set off again for
Galilee. He wished to go back there for it was there he
had spoken of how a prophet is given no honour in his

own country: now, the Galileans made him welcome, for they had gone up to Jerusalem like himself at the time of the feast and had seen all the things he did there.

So he came again to Cana in Galilee, where he had turned the water into wine.

3. The Living Word

A nobleman, one of the court officials, had a son lying sick at Capharnaum. This man, when he heard that Jesus had come from Judaea into Galilee, went to him and begged him to come down from Cana and heal the child, for he was at the point of death. Jesus said:

> Unless you see wonders and prodigies, all of you,
>> you refuse to believe.

But the nobleman answered only:

> Sir, come down
>> or my little son will die.

Jesus said to him:

> Go in peace:
>> your son is cured.[1]

The man believed what Jesus told him, and set off on his journey home. On the way down the hillside his servants met him, bringing word that his son was alive and well. He asked them when the child had begun to mend. They told him: Yesterday afternoon, at one o'clock, the fever left him. The father realized it was at this same hour that

[1] cf. p. 83n.

Jesus had said to him, Your son is cured. And he gave his faith wholly to Jesus, and all his household with him.
So a second time Jesus gave a sign to the people of Galilee on his return from Judaea.

After this, Jesus went up again to Jerusalem for one of the festivals of the Jews. There is in the city, close by the Sheep Gate, a pool called in Hebrew Bezatha, with five porches built about it. Under these porches would lie a great number of sick people—blind, lame, disabled—waiting for the moment when the waters would be stirred up by a fresh inflow.[1] One man was lying there who for thirty-eight years had been crippled with disease. Jesus, seeing him, and knowing he had been disabled a long time, asked him: Do you truly want to be cured?
Sir, replied the cripple, I have no one to help me down into the pool when the waters are stirred up; and so before I can reach them another has gone down ahead of me.
Jesus said to him:
  Stand up: pick up your bed: and walk.
Straightway the man was restored to wholeness of body; he picked up his bed, and walked.[2]
This took place on the sabbath; and the Jews said to the man who had been cured:
  It is the sabbath day:[3]
    the law forbids you to carry your bed.
He answered:
  The man who cured my body told me:

[1] cf. p. 73n[2].   [2] cf. pp. 64, 102–3.   [3] cf. pp. 72 *sqq.*

153

Pick up your bed, and walk.
They asked him:
    And who is this man?
But the cripple who had been cured did not know.
Meanwhile Jesus had withdrawn from the crowd which
thronged the place. Later, however, he found the man in
the temple and said to him:
    Now that you are made whole again in body
      keep yourself from sin
        lest some worse evil befall you.
Then the man went back and told the Jews it was Jesus
who had cured him. That was why the Jews stirred up ill
will against him, because he did such things on the sabbath. So he began to ask them:[1]
    Why do you want to kill me?
They cried:
    You are possessed:
      who wants to kill you?
Jesus answered:
    Moses gave you the law
      but you do not keep the truth of the law
        and so because of one work of mine
          you are astounded.
    Moses gave you the law of circumcision—
      though this comes not from him
               but from the patriarchs—
    and so you are ready to circumcise on the sabbath
      that Moses' law may not be broken:
    what right then have you to be indignant with me

---

[1] The next nineteen lines correspond to 7^{19b-24}.

for giving health to the whole man on the sabbath?
Do not make shallow judgements.
  Look to what lies beneath the surface,
    and so make your judgements just.
  My Father's activity is unceasing;
    and as he does,
      so must I do.

At this they became all the more determined to kill him
since he not only broke the sabbath but also spoke of God
as his Father, making himself equal to God.
Jesus therefore said again:
  I tell you truly:
    the Son can do nothing as coming from himself:
    he can do only what he sees his Father doing.
      What the Father does
        the Son will also do.
      For the Father loves the Son
        and shows him all that he himself does.
      Far greater things than these you have seen
        will he show him
          so that you will be filled with wonder.
      Just as the Father raises men from the dead
        and gives them life again,
          so does the Son give life to whom he will.
      All judgement also the Father has left to the Son[1]
        while he himself passes judgement on no man,
          that all may honour the Son
            as they honour the Father.

[1] cf. p. 71.

To deny honour to the Son
　is to deny honour to the Father who sent him.

I tell you truly:
　he who listens to my words
　　and gives himself wholly in faith
　　　to him who sent me
　　already has within him
　　　the life which is eternal.
　He need have no fear of being judged:
　　already he has passed from death into life.

I tell you truly:
　the hour is coming,
　　is indeed already come,
　when those who are dead in spirit
　　will hear the voice of God's Son,
　and those who listen and take heed shall live.
For as the Father has within him the source of life,
　so he has given to the Son
　　　　　　to have within him the source of life.
And he has given him authority to judge mankind
　since he is the Son of Man.
Do not marvel at this:
　there are greater marvels yet.
For the hour will come
　when all who lie in the tomb
　　shall come forth at the sound of his voice:
　those whose lives have been good
　　shall rise up into life;

those whose lives have been evil
shall rise to receive their judgement.

I can do nothing as coming from myself:
I judge as my Father bids me judge,
and so my judgement is just,
since it is not my own will I follow
but the will of him who sent me.

If I testify on my own behalf to the truth of what I say,
that testimony is of no avail.
But there is another who testifies for me
and his testimony I know to be worthy of trust.
You yourselves sent messengers to John
to inquire about me
and he testified to the truth.
Not that I lean on any human testimony:
it is for your own good I remind you of this:
John was a lamp burning and shining
to show you the way,
and you were willing enough
to sun yourselves for a season
in his light.
He did indeed testify on my behalf.
But I have a testimony greater than that of John:
the work my Father empowered me to do,
the work I am now doing,
bears me witness that it was the Father who sent me;
and the Father himself, who sent me,
bears witness for me.

But you will not accept his word.
For in refusing to believe in his messenger
  you have shut your ears to the sound of his voice,
  you have shut your eyes to any revealing of him;
you cannot even claim that his words live in your hearts
  (those words of the scriptures over which you pore,
  thinking to find there the life which is eternal)
for it is these same words which bear witness to me
  and you will not come to me
    to find life in me.

Do not think this means I seek glory from men:
  it means I know what is in your hearts;
        I know it is not love of God
          nor zeal to defend his sovereign glory
          that moves you to act as you do:
I come to you in my Father's name
  and you will not welcome me,
yet if another come to you
  with no name to bear witness to him but his own,
  him you will welcome.
How indeed could you believe,
  you who exult in the praise
    you receive from one another
  and have no concern for the glory
    given only by God?

But do not think I will make accusations against you
  to my Father:
you have your accuser already:

Moses,
   the man in whom you put your trust.
He is your accuser
   since if you really believed him
      you would believe in me:
         it was of me he wrote.
   If you will not believe his writings
      how can you believe in my words?

4. *The Living Bread*

A little while before the great Jewish festival of the pasch,
Jesus crossed over the sea of Galilee or Tiberias. But as a
great crowd followed him, because of the signs they had
seen him perform over the sick, he climbed up the hillside, and there sat down with his disciples.

The crowd, however, soon gathered around him. Jesus,
looking up and seeing this, said to Philip: Where are we
to buy bread for all these? (He said this to test Philip's
trust in him: he himself knew what he was going to do.)
Philip answered: Two hundred silver pieces would not
buy bread enough, even if each one took only a little.
Andrew, one of the disciples, the brother of Simon Peter,
said: There is a boy here who has five barley loaves and
two fishes; but what good is that among so many people?
Jesus said: Tell them to sit down.

There was plenty of grass where they were.

So the people sat down; there were about five thousand
of them. Jesus took the loaves, and gave thanks. Then he

distributed the bread, and the fishes too, and all ate as much as they wanted. When their hunger was fully satisfied he said to his disciples: Gather up the fragments left over, that nothing be wasted. They did so; and with these fragments left over from the five barley loaves they filled twelve baskets.[1]

The people, seeing this sign which Jesus had performed, began to say: Truly this must be the prophet who is to come into the world.

So Jesus, knowing they had a mind to carry him off and make a king of him, withdrew further into the hillside, quite alone.

When evening had come the disciples went down to the lake and, getting into a boat, began to cross over to Capharnaum.

Darkness fell.

Jesus had not come back to them. A strong wind was blowing; the sea was growing rough. When they had rowed some three or four miles, suddenly they saw Jesus walking on the water and coming towards the boat. They were filled with terror. But he said to them: It is I: do not be afraid.[2] Then they made to help him on board; but at once the boat reached land at the point they were making for.

Next morning the crowd was still waiting on the other side of the lake. They knew there had been only one boat there, and that Jesus had not embarked with his disciples but had let them cross over without him. In the meantime,

[1] cf. pp. 64 *sqq.*   [2] cf. p. 33n.

however, other boats from Tiberias had put in near the
place where they ate the bread after the Lord had given
thanks. So, seeing that neither Jesus nor his disciples
were there, they took these boats and made for Capharnaum to look for Jesus.

There they found him; and they asked him:

Master, when did you come here?

Jesus said to them:

I tell you truly:
you have been looking for me
not because you saw the signs I did
and welcomed them as signs
but because you were given your fill of bread.
You ought to be working
not for the food that perishes
but for the food that remains, unperishing,
and brings you to the life which is eternal.
You ought to be working
for the food the Son of Man can give you
since God, the Father, has given him
power and authority to do so.

They asked him:

What then are the works God would have us do?

He answered:

One work God asks of you:
an enduring faith in him whom he has sent.

They said:

But what sign can you show us
that will make us believe you?
What work do you yourself accomplish?

Can you excel that of Moses?
For of the manna our fathers ate in the desert
it is written:
He gave them bread from heaven for their food.
Jesus answered:
I tell you truly:
what Moses gave you
was not the bread coming from heaven:
the bread that is truly from heaven
is given only by my Father.
It is that bread,
God's bread,
which comes from heaven
and gives life to the world.
They said to him:
Then, Lord, give us always of this bread.
Jesus answered:
I AM the bread of life.
He who comes to me shall never go hungry;
he who puts his faith in me shall never know thirst.
All those the Father has given into my care
will come to me;
and those who come to me
I will never turn away.
I have come down from heaven
not to do my own will
but to do the will of him who sent me;
and this is the will of him who sent me:
that I should lose none of those
he has given into my care

but should raise them up at the last day.
This is my Father's will:
  that all who see the Son for what he is,
    and so put their faith in him,
      shall have within them
        the life which is eternal,
and that I shall raise them up at the last day.
But you, as I told you before,
  even though you have seen me,
    still you will not put your faith in me.

The Jews were now murmuring against him because he
had said he was the bread that comes down from heaven.
They said one to another:
  Is he not Jesus son of Joseph,
    whose father and mother we know well?
  How can he say he came down from heaven?
Jesus said to them:
  Do not murmur.
  No one can come to me
    unless the Father, who sent me,
      draw him to me.
  It is written in the book of the prophets:
    They shall all be taught by God.
  Whoever has listened to the Father
    and learnt from him
      will come to me:
  and I will raise him up at the last day.
  Not that anyone has seen the Father
    save him who comes from God;

he has seen the Father.
But in truth I tell you:
  he who has faith
    has within him the life which is eternal.

I AM the bread of life.
  Your fathers who ate manna in the desert
  are dead;
this bread comes down from heaven
  that he who eats of it
    may never die.
I AM this living bread
  coming down from heaven:
    he who eats of it
      shall live for ever.
This bread I am to give
  is my flesh,
    given for the world,
    to give life to the world.

These words led the Jews to argue hotly among themselves. How can this man give us his flesh to eat? they asked.

Jesus said to them:
  I tell you truly:
    if you do not eat the flesh of the Son of Man
    and drink his blood[1]
      you cannot have life in you.

[1] cf. pp. 67 *sqq.*

He who eats my flesh and drinks my blood
　has within him the life which is eternal,
　　and I will raise him up at the last day.
For my flesh is true food,
　my blood is true drink:
　　and he who eats my flesh
　　　and drinks my blood
　　　　lives in me
　　　　　and I in him.
As I live by the life given me by the Father,
　the living Father who sent me,
　so will he who eats me
　live by the life given him by me.
This is what the bread from heaven means.
　Your fathers in the desert
　　ate of a different bread, the manna,
　　　and they are dead;
　　he who eats of this bread
　　　shall live for ever.

All this Jesus said, teaching in the synagogue at Capharnaum. And many of his disciples, when they heard him,
said:
　This is a strange, crude doctrine:
　who could bring himself to accept it?[1]
Jesus knew in his own mind they were murmuring
against his teaching.
He said to them:
　Is this a stumbling-block to your faith?

[1] cf. p. 67.

What then will you think—
  you who think always according to the flesh,
                          not the spirit—[1]
if you see the Son of Man being lifted up
  and going up to the place where he was before?
Only the spirit gives life;
  the lifeless flesh is of no avail.
The words I spoke to you are spirit,
  the words I spoke to you are life for you:
    yet some among you lack the faith to hear them.
Jesus said this because from the beginning he knew
  who would not believe in him
    and who would betray him.
And he added:
  That is why I told you
    no one can come to me
  unless it is given him by the Father to do so.
After this many of his disciples left him and would have
no more to do with him, but went back to their old ways.
Then Jesus said to the twelve:
  And you, will you too go away from me?
Simon Peter answered him:
  Lord, to whom should we go?
    You have the words which give life,
      the secret of the life which is eternal;
        and we believe,
          we know,
      that you are the Holy One of God.
Jesus said:

[1] cf. *infra* 8[15], *supra* pp. 64–6.

Did I not choose you,
 all of you,
  my twelve?
Yet one of you is a devil.
He meant Judas son of Simon of Kerioth:
  he, one of the twelve,
   was to betray him.

5. *Plottings of the Blind*

After this, Jesus went about in Galilee; he would not go
into Judaea since the Jews were determined to kill him.
But as the Jewish feast of Tabernacles drew near his kins-
men said to him:
 You ought to leave Galilee and go into Judaea
  so that your followers there may see
   the works you do.
 A man who wants to become well known
  does not let his deeds remain hidden.
 If you do these works you must want to become well
                                                known:
  go and show yourself, then, to the world at large.
(Even his close kinsmen had no true faith in him.)
Jesus said to them:
 The time for that is not yet come.
  You may shape your plans as you will:
   I must follow the plan laid down by my Father.
  You are free: the world cannot hate you
   since it is of one mind with you.

But the world does hate me
  since I bear witness that its works are evil.
Do you then go up for the feast.
  I will not go up with you
    since my time is not yet come.

And having said this he stayed behind in Galilee. But later, when his kinsfolk had already left for the feast, he too went up to Jerusalem, but secretly, as though he would not be seen.[1] Meanwhile the Jews were looking about for him during the festival, and asking: Where is he? And there was much whispering about him in the crowds. Some said: He is a good man. Others said: No, he is leading the people astray. But no one dared speak openly about him for fear of the Jews.

Then, half-way through the festival, Jesus went up into the temple and began to teach.
The Jews were astonished:
  How did the man pick up this learning? they asked.
  He was never schooled by the rabbis.
Jesus said:
  My teaching is not of my own devising:
    it comes from him who sent me.
  Any man who loves God's will
    and tries to follow it
  will know whether my teaching comes from God
    or is of my own making.
  For the man whose teaching is of his own making
    seeks glory for himself;

[1] cf. p. 14.

but the man who seeks glory only for him who sent him
has no dishonesty in him,
  and his teaching is true.

Meanwhile some of the people of Jerusalem were saying:
  Is not this the man the rulers are plotting to kill?
    Yet here he is, speaking openly,
      and they say nothing to him:
    can it be they are convinced
      he is the Christ?
    But when the Christ comes
      no one is to know where he comes from,
        whereas we know well
            where this man comes from.
Then Jesus, who was teaching in the temple, cried:
  You do indeed know me, and whence I come.
    Yet I am come not of my own will
      but because I was sent,
        sent by one who has the right to send:
      and him you do not know.
    I do know him
      because I come from him:
        it was he who sent me.

At this they would have seized hold of him. But in fact
no one touched him, for his hour had not yet come. And
among the people many put their faith in him; for they
said:
  Can we expect the Christ, at his coming,
    to show us more signs than this man has shown?

When the pharisees heard of these whisperings among
the crowd, they and the chief priests sent guards to arrest
him.

Then Jesus said:

   Only for a little while now shall I be with you
     and then I go back to him who sent me.
    You will seek for me
      but you will not find me,
    for you cannot come to the place where I live.

The Jews said one to another:

        Where can this place be
         to which he is going
          and we cannot go?
   Will he go to the Jews living abroad
         among the Greeks
    so as to teach the Greeks?[1]
   How can he say we shall seek and not find him
    and where he is going we cannot go?

On the last, most solemn day of the festival Jesus stood up
and cried:

   If any man thirst
    let him come to me;
    let him drink,
   if he have faith in me;
   for it is of me that the scripture says:
    from within him shall spring up
     fountains of living water.

By this water he meant the Spirit

              [1] cf. p. 84.

who would be given to those who believed in him:
  as yet the Spirit had not been given
    since Jesus had not yet been
      raised to glory.[1]

Some of the people, when they heard his words, said:
  This must be the great prophet.
Others said:
  He is the Christ.
But others argued:
  Can the Christ come from Galilee?
    Do not the scriptures say he is to come
      from David's stock and
         David's city, Bethlehem?
So the crowd were at odds because of him. And some
would have laid hands on him; but again no one in fact
touched him.

Meanwhile the guards had gone back to the chief priests
and pharisees.
These asked them:
  Why have you not brought him to us?
They answered:
  Never man spoke as this man speaks.
The pharisees retorted:
  Have you too been led astray?
  Look among the rulers and pharisees:
    is there a single one who believes in him?

[1] cf. p. 27n[2].

As for this rabble, who know nothing of the law,
  they are accursed.
Then Nicodemus—
  he who had come to Jesus by night—
    although he was one of them, said to them:
  Is it the way of our law
    to condemn a man without a hearing,
      without first finding the facts?
They answered:
  Are you perhaps from Galilee also?
    Study the scriptures:
      you will find
        no prophet ever comes from Galilee.
And they went off, each to his own home.

8^{12} Once again Jesus spoke to them all. He said to them:
  I AM the light of the world.
    He who becomes my follower
      shall never walk in darkness:
        he will have within him
          the light that is life.
The pharisees broke in:
  You are testifying on your own behalf:
    that is not valid testimony.
Jesus answered:
  Yes, I am testifying on my own behalf,
    nevertheless my testimony is indeed valid
      because I know where I came from
          and where I am going
      whereas you do not know.

You, when you pass judgement,
  judge simply by appearances,
    by the flesh your fleshly eyes can see.
I do not now pass judgement on any man,
  but if I did, my judgement would be true,
    for I do not stand alone:
    my Father, who sent me, is with me:
and it is laid down in your law
  that if two bear witness together
    their word shall stand.
  Yes, I do testify on my own behalf;
  but my Father who sent me
    testifies for me too.
They retorted:
  And where is this father of yours?
Jesus said:
  You know neither me nor my Father.
  If you knew me
    you would know my Father too.

All these things Jesus said in the treasury, while he was
teaching in the temple. And still no man laid hands on
him, for his hour had not yet come.

Again he said to them:
  I am going away,
    and you will look for me, later on,
      but you will not find me,
        for where I am going
          you cannot come.

173

You will not find me
and so must die in your sin,
the sin of rejecting me now.

At this the Jews began to say:
Does he mean he will kill himself
when he says,
Where I am going
you cannot come?

But Jesus went on:
You are earthy:
you belong to this world here below.
I do not belong to this world:
I am from heaven.
That is why I said you must die in your sin:
you shall indeed die in your sin
unless you believe that
I AM.
They said:
But who are you?
He answered:
I AM what I have told you from the beginning.[1]
For the present you must know me through my words.
I could indeed say much concerning you,
much to condemn you,
but no, I tell the world
only what I have been told
by him who sent me.

[1] cf. p. 41n.

And what he says is true.
(They did not grasp that he meant the Father.)
Jesus went on:

    Later, when you have lifted up the Son of Man,
        then you will realize
          that I AM.
        You will realize
         that I do nothing of my own will.
        You will realize
         that in saying these things
        I say only what the Father has taught me.
He who sent me has not left me alone:
  he is always with me
    since I do always what he wills.

Because he said this, many among the Jews were drawn
to believe in Jesus. To these he said:

    If you live according to my teaching,
    if you are faithful to my word I have given you,
      you will be truly my disciples:
        then you will understand the truth
         and the truth will set you free.
But to this they answered:

    We are of Abraham's stock;
    we have never been slaves to any man:
      how can you say we shall be set free?
Jesus said:

    I tell you truly:
      every man who lives in sin
        is the slave of sin.

A slave cannot count on living for ever
  in his master's home;
only the son of the house knows it is
        always his home;
only, then, if the Son makes free men of you
  will you in truth be free.
I know you are of Abraham's stock;
  nevertheless you seek to kill me
    because my words find no entry into your hearts:
    my words tell of what I have seen
      in the house of my Father;
      your deeds tell of what you have heard
      in the house of your father.
They said:
  But our father is Abraham.
Jesus answered:
  If you were trueborn children of Abraham
    you would follow Abraham's example.
  But you seek to kill me
    who tell you the truth
      as God has told it to me:
  that is not what Abraham did.
    No, the example you follow
      is that of your true father.
They cried:
  We are no offspring of infidelity:
    God, and God only, is our father.
Jesus answered:
  Were God your father you would love me,
    for I came forth from God

to live amongst you.
It was not of my own will that I came:
  it was he who sent me.
Why is it you do not understand my language?
It is because you cannot bear to hear my message,
                        the word I bring you,
            and you cannot bear it because
                you belong to your father,
                your desire is to fulfil his desires:
            and your father is the devil.
He, in the beginning, brought death to man;
  and never, from the beginning,
    did he speak a word rooted in truth,
      for there is no truth in him:
    when he speaks falsehood
    he is but speaking his own idiom:
      for he is falsehood
      and begets falsehood.
As for me, it is because I speak the truth to you
  that you will not believe me.
There is not one among you who,
  by convicting me of sin,
    can convict me of falsehood.
If, then, I speak truth, not falsehood,
  why do you refuse to believe me?

    Those who are born of God
        and belong to God
      hear the words of God:
    it is because you are not born of God

and do not belong to God
that you do not hear my word.

At this the Jews cried:
  We were right:
    you are a Samaritan;
    you are possessed.
Jesus answered:
  I am not possessed.
  I speak as I do,
    not because I obey a devil's bidding
    but because I honour my Father and his bidding.
  And though you seek to dishonour me
    I do not concern myself with that
      for I do not seek glory for myself;
  there is another whose concern that is,
    and who will be the judge.

  I tell you truly:
    if any man live according to my word
    he will not see death for ever.

The Jews said:
  Now we are sure you are possessed:
    Abraham is dead,
    the prophets are dead,
  and yet you say
    if any man live according to your word
    he will never taste death.

Are you then greater than our father Abraham,
who is dead,
and the prophets, who are dead?
Who do you think you are?
Jesus answered:
Were I to glorify myself
the glory would be vain.
It is my Father who glorifies me,
he whom you glory in claiming as your God,
known to you alone,
though in truth you do not know him.
I do know him:
were I to say otherwise
I would be like you,
a liar.
I do know him:
and I carry out his bidding.
You claim Abraham as your father:
Abraham exulted at the thought of seeing
the Day of the Lord,
my day:
he saw it,
and was filled with joy.
The Jews cried out:
You are not yet fifty
and you have seen Abraham?
Jesus answered:
I tell you truly:
before Abraham was born
I AM.

At this they took up stones, to kill him.[1] But Jesus hid himself from them and withdrew to the mount of Olives.

Then, early next morning, he came again into the temple. The people all gathered about him, and he sat down and began to teach them. But now the scribes and pharisees brought to him a woman who had been caught in the act of adultery.[2] Making her stand out in full view of all they said to him:

> Master, this woman has just been caught
> in the very act of adultery:
> Moses laid it down in his law
> that such should be stoned to death:
> but you, what do you say?

They asked him this to set a trap for him, hoping to find a charge to bring against him. But Jesus simply bent down and began to write on the ground with his finger. Then, as they continued to question him, he looked up and said to them:

> Whichever of you has never sinned,
> let him throw the first stone at her.

Then he bent down again and went on writing.
And one by one they began to go out, starting with the eldest, till there was no one left with Jesus but the woman, still standing out in full view.
Jesus, looking up, asked her:

> Where are they? Has no one condemned you?

She answered:

---

[1] This and the next thirty lines correspond to 8[59, 1-11].
[2] cf. pp. 77–8.

No one, Lord.
He said to her:
    Nor do I condemn you.
        Go home now, and sin no more.

6. *Light and Shepherd of the World*

9   Then, as he went on his way, he saw a man who had been
blind from birth.[1]
His disciples asked him:
    Master, who was guilty of sin,
      this man or his parents,
        that he was born blind?[2]
Jesus answered:
    It was not for any sin of his,
      or of his parents,
        that he was born blind:
    it was in order that through him
      the works of God·might be shown forth.
    Whilst the daylight lasts for us
      we must carry out the work of him who sent me;
    soon the night will come upon us,
      the night when one can work no longer;
    but for as long as I am in the world
      I am the light of the world.

When he had said this, Jesus spat on the ground, made
clay with the spittle, and rubbed it on the man's eyes.

[1] cf. pp. 73 *sqq.*   [2] cf. p. 73.

Then he said to him: Go now and wash in the pool of
Siloe. (This name means One who is Sent.) The man
went, and washed, and when he came back he could see.
The neighbours, and those who had been used to seeing
him begging, said to one another: Is not this the man
who used to sit here begging?
Some said: Yes, it is. Others replied: No, it is another man
who looks like him.
Then he himself told them:

I am the man.

They asked him:

How is it then that your eyes have been opened?

He answered:

The man called Jesus made clay
and rubbed it on my eyes
and told me to go and wash in the pool of Siloe:
I went, and washed, and now I can see.

They asked him:

Where is he?

But he said:

I do not know.

Then they brought him before the pharisees.

Now this day, when Jesus made the clay and opened the
man's eyes, was the sabbath. The pharisees in their turn
asked the man how he had gained his sight.
He told them:

He put clay on my eyes;
I washed;
and I can see.

Some of the pharisees said:
  The man cannot be from God:
    he breaks the sabbath.
But others among them asked:
  How could a sinner do signs such as these?
And they were at odds.
So, turning again to the man, they asked him:
  And you, what have you to say of him,
    since it was your eyes he opened?
The man answered:
  He is a prophet.

But now the Jews refused to believe his story till they had
summoned and questioned his parents.
They asked them:
  Is this your son, who you say was born blind?
    If so, how is it that he can see?
His parents answered:
  We know this is our son
    and that he was born blind;
   but how it is he can see
    or who opened his eyes
      we do not know:
    he is of age: let him speak for himself.
They said this because they were afraid of the Jews, who
had agreed to expel from the synagogue anyone who
acknowledged Jesus to be the Christ.
So once again the Jews summoned the man who had been
blind. They solemnly adjured him to tell the truth; then
they said to him:

We know now beyond a doubt
  that this man is a sinner.
He replied:
  Whether or not he is a sinner
    I do not know:
      it is not for me to say.
    All I know is this:
      I was blind,
        and now I see.
They asked him yet again:
  What was it he did?
  How did he open your eyes?
He answered:
  I told you that before
    and you would not listen;
  why must you hear it again and again?
  Would you become his disciples?
This roused them to fury. They became abusive:
  It is you who are his disciple.
  We are disciples of Moses.
  We know God spoke to Moses;
    as for this man, we know nothing of him,
      not even where he comes from.
He said to them:
  That is what is so amazing:
  that you should have no idea
          where he comes from
  and yet he opened my eyes.
  We know beyond a doubt God does not listen
    to sinners' prayers;

but if a man is devout and does God's will,
   to him God listens.
  Never since the world began
   has any man been known
    to open the eyes of one born blind:
  if this man were not from God
   he could achieve nothing.
They cried out:
  From birth you have been steeped in sin,
   and will you teach us our lessons?
And they threw him out.

When Jesus heard they had done this he went to find
him, and asked him:
  Do you believe in the Son of Man?
He answered:
  Lord, tell me who he is,
   that I may believe in him.
Jesus said to him:
  Your eyes have seen him.
   He is talking to you.
The man said:
  Lord, I give you my faith.
And falling to his knees he worshipped him.

Then Jesus said:
  So must my coming into the world
   bring a judgement on the world:
    those who humbly confess their blindness
     are given sight;

those who pride themselves on their vision
    become yet blinder than before.[1]
There were some pharisees among those who stood about
Jesus listening to him.
These asked him:
    You would not say that we, too, are blind?
Jesus answered:
    If you were blind and humbly confessed your blindness
      you would be without sin;
    but no, you claim to see clearly,
      so you cannot escape your sin.

10   I tell you truly:
    a man who enters the sheepfold
      not through the door
        but by climbing in elsewhere
          comes to rob and plunder.
    The shepherd, who cares for the sheep,
      enters through the door.
    At his coming the keeper of the door throws it open.
      And the sheep listen to his voice:
        he calls his own sheep, one by one,
          by name,
        and they come out to him;
    and when he has brought them all out
      he walks in front of them,
        and they follow him
        for they know his voice.
    But if a stranger comes

[1] cf. pp. 70 *sqq.*

they will not follow him,
they run away from him,
  for his voice they do not know.

Thus Jesus spoke to them in symbol; but they could not
grasp his meaning.
So he went on:
  I tell you truly:
    I AM the door of the sheepfold.[1]
    Those who climb in elsewhere
      are robbers and plunderers:
    to them the sheep will not listen.
    I AM the door.
      He who enters in through me will be
        safe and sound:
      he can come and go as he will,
        freely,
      and will find pasture for his sheep.
      The robber comes only to steal, to kill,
                              to destroy;
      I am come that the sheep may have life,
        rich and full and abounding.
    I AM the good shepherd.[2]
      The good shepherd
        lays down his life for his sheep.
      The hired man,
        who works for a wage but is no true shepherd,
        has no real care for the sheep
        since they are not his own;

          [1] cf. p. 50.   [2] cf. p. 79.

so, when he sees the wolf coming,
  he abandons the sheep and runs off,
  and the wolf harries the sheep
     and scatters them.
I AM the good shepherd.
 I know my own sheep, lovingly,
  each of them by name,
  and they know me,
 just as the Father knows me
  and I know the Father.
 And I lay down my life for my sheep.
Other sheep I have,
 not of this fold:
 I must lead them to pasture, too,
  (and they will listen to my voice):
 so there will be but one flock
  and one shepherd.

For this my Father loves me:
 that I lay down my life
  to take it up again afterwards.
 I lay it down of my own accord:
  no man can rob me of it.
 I have the power to lay it down,
  the power to take it up again:
for that is what my Father charged me to do.

At these words discord broke out afresh among the Jews.
Some of them said:

He is possessed.
He is out of his mind.
  Why do you listen to him?
Others said:
  These are not the words of one possessed;
    and could a devil open the eyes of the blind?

The feast of the dedication of the temple came round.
It was winter-time.
Jesus was in the temple, walking to and fro in Solomon's
porch. The Jews, seeing him there, surrounded him and
said to him:
  How long are you going to keep us on tenterhooks?
  If you are really the Christ, tell us so:
    have done with veiled words:
      speak out openly.
Jesus answered:
  I have already told you
    but you will not believe me.
  All the works I do in my Father's name
    speak for me
      but still you will not believe me.
  And you will not believe
    because you are not sheep of my flock.
  My own sheep listen to me,
    recognize my voice,
      and so I know they are truly mine.
  My own sheep follow me,
    and I give them life, the life eternal:
      therefore they will never be lost,

    no one can snatch them from me,
      they are safe in my hands for ever;
      for no one has power like that of my Father
        who gave them to me;
        no one can snatch anything from his hands;
        and I and the Father are one.

At this the Jews again took up stones, to kill him.
But Jesus said to them:
    Many works of mercy I have done in your sight
      as my Father empowered me to do:
      for which of these would you stone me?
They answered:
    It is not for any work of mercy we would stone you.
    It is for blasphemy:
    you are but a man,
      yet you claim to be God.

Jesus said to them:
    Is it not written, in your scriptures,
      of the judges of God's people:
      I have said, You are gods?
    If the scriptures call these men gods—
      and the scriptures are not to be gainsaid—
    what of him whom God has dedicated
      and sent into the world?
      Will you accuse him of blasphemy
        for calling himself the Son of God?
    If the work I do is not the work of my Father

do not put your faith in me;
but if it is the work of my Father
then, though you will not believe
because of my words
you must believe
because of my works:
so you will see, and be convinced,
that the Father does live in me
and I in him.

When they heard this they again would have laid hands
on him. But he escaped from them and went back across
the Jordan to the place where John had first baptized.
There he remained for some time.

And many came to him there. For they said: John did not
perform any signs, but all he told us of this man has
proved to be true. And many of them put their faith in
Jesus.

7. *Death and Life in Duel*

In the village of Bethany a man named Lazarus had fallen
ill. He was the brother of Martha and Mary, that Mary
who anointed the Lord with sweet-smelling oils and
wiped his feet with her hair.

The two sisters now sent word to Jesus, saying:
Lord, your friend is ill.[1]

[1] cf. pp. 80 *sqq.*

When he heard this, Jesus sent back answer:
  This illness is not to end in death
    but in the revealing of God's glory
      through the glorifying of God's Son.
So, although he loved Martha and her sister and Lazarus,
Jesus stayed where he was for two days after hearing the
news; only then did he say to his disciples:
  Let us go back into Judaea.
At this they cried:
  But, Master, only a short while ago
    the Jews would have stoned you to death:
  would you now go back amongst them?
Jesus answered:
  In the day's course
    there are but twelve hours of daylight.[1]
  A man who walks in the daytime does not stumble
    for the world's light gives sight to his eyes;
  when darkness has fallen, then he stumbles,
    for the night takes the sight from his eyes.
As they remained silent he went on:
  Lazarus our friend has fallen asleep:
  I will go and wake him.
The disciples said:
  But, Lord, if he is sleeping he will get better.
For they thought Jesus was talking of natural sleep; but
it was death he meant. So then he told them plainly:
  Lazarus is dead.
  And for your sake I am glad I was not there,
    for now your faith may be made the stronger.

[1] cf. p. 80n[2].

Come, let us go to him.

Then Thomas—the name means The Twin[1]—said to the others:

    Yes, let us go with him
      and meet death with him.

When Jesus arrived he found it was the fourth day since the burial of Lazarus.[2] Bethany is not far from Jerusalem, about two miles, and many Jews had come out there to comfort Martha and Mary over the loss of their brother. Martha, when she heard Jesus had come, went out to meet him, while Mary stayed behind in the house. Martha said to him:

    Lord, had you been here
      my brother would not have died.
    Yet even now, I know,
      whatever you asked of God
        he would grant it you.[3]

Jesus said to her:

    Your brother will rise again.

Martha answered:

    I know that he will rise again
      at the resurrection on the last day.

Jesus said:

        I AM resurrection,
          here and now,
            because I AM life.
        He who believes in me,
          if he die, shall live again;

[1] cf. pp. 113–14.   [2] cf. p. 80.   [3] cf. p. 82.

and all who live,
  if they have faith in me,
    shall never die.
  Do you believe this?
She told him:
  Yes, Lord, I believe this.
  I believe
    that you are the Messiah,
              the Son of God,
              he for whose coming
                the world has been waiting.

Then she went back to fetch her sister Mary. She whispered to her:
  The Master is here
    and would see you.
Mary got up at once and went to him. As yet he had not reached the village but was still at the place where Martha had met him. The Jews who were in the house with Mary, comforting her, when they saw how she got up quickly and went out, followed her: they thought she was going to the tomb, to weep there. Mary came to the place where Jesus was; and when she saw him she fell at his feet saying:
  Lord, had you been here
    my brother would not have died.
When Jesus saw how she and those who had come with her were weeping he was deeply troubled in spirit, so that he groaned with grief and anger.[1]

[1] cf. pp. 83–4.

He asked them:

Where have you buried him?

They said to him:

Lord, come and see.

Jesus began to weep. The Jews said: See how he loved him. But some of them added: Could not he, who opened the eyes of the blind man, have prevented this man's death?

Jesus came to the tomb. It was a cave;[1] a stone had been put over the mouth of it.

He groaned again; then he told them:

Take away the stone.

Martha said to him:

Lord, it is the fourth day:

by now the air will be foul.

Jesus said to her:

Did I not tell you

that if you believed

you would see God's glory

shown forth through God's power?

So they took away the stone. Jesus, lifting up his eyes to heaven, said:

Father, I thank you for hearing my prayer.

I know that you hear me always,

but I say this for the sake of

those standing here with me,

that they may believe that you have sent me.

Then he cried in a loud voice:

Lazarus, come out from the tomb.

[1] cf. p. 54.

And the dead man came out, his arms and legs still bound in the linen grave-bands, his face still covered with a cloth.

Jesus said to them:

Loose him, and let him go home.

As a result of this, many of the Jews, those who had come to Mary and had seen what Jesus did, believed in him. But others ran to the pharisees to tell them about it; and the chief priests and pharisees at once called together a council.

What are we about? they asked. This man performs many signs: if we let him go on unchecked the whole people will believe in him, and then the Romans will come and destroy our holy place and our very life as a nation.

But one of them, Caiphas, who was high priest in that year, cried:

Have you no sense?

Can you not see

it is better for one man to die for the people

than for the whole nation to perish?

He did not say this on his own initiative. As high priest in that year it was given him to prophesy that Jesus would die for the nation, and not just for that one nation but that all God's children, scattered far and wide, should be gathered into one fold.

From that day then they plotted how to kill Jesus. He, for this reason, no longer went about openly among the

Jews, but withdrew into the countryside, to a city called
Ephrem, on the edge of the desert; and there he remained with his disciples.

When the Jewish feast of the pasch was close at hand
many of the country people went up to Jerusalem for the
ritual cleansing before the feast. There they looked for
Jesus; and as they stood about in the temple they asked
one another: What do you think? Will he come up for the
feast or not?
For the chief priests and pharisees had given orders that
anyone who knew where Jesus was should inform them,
that they might arrest him.

Then, six days before the pasch, Jesus went to Bethany
where Lazarus lived, the man he had brought back to
life. There a feast was given in his honour: Martha
served at table; Lazarus was among the guests. And
Mary brought a pound-pot of costly sweet-smelling oils
made from pure spikenard, and she poured it all out over
the feet of Jesus and then wiped them with her hair: the
whole house was filled with the scent.
One of the disciples, Judas of Kerioth, the one who was to
betray him, said: Why were these oils not sold? They
were worth three hundred silver pieces, which could
have been given to the poor.
But it was not concern for the poor that made him say
this: he was a thief: he had charge of the common purse
and took for himself what was put into it.

Jesus said:

Leave her alone.
She kept these oils
to prepare me for my burial.
The poor you have always among you:
you will not always have me.

Meanwhile those Jews who had been looking for Jesus
learned that he was at Bethany. So they went out there,
hoping thus to see both Jesus himself and also Lazarus
whom he had brought back from the dead. This made the
chief priests resolve to kill Lazarus as well, since so many
of the Jews were deserting them because of him, and
giving their faith to Jesus.

Then, on the day after the supper given for Jesus,
the crowds who had gone up to Jerusalem for the
festival heard that he was coming into the city. So they
went out to meet him, carrying palm-branches,[1] and
shouting:

Hosanna!
Blessed be he who comes to us in the Lord's name,
and is Israel's king.

Jesus, finding a little donkey,[2] mounted it. Thus he fulfilled those words of the scriptures:

Do not be afraid, daughter of Sion:
see, your king comes to you
riding on an ass's foal.

At the time, the disciples did not understand these events;

[1] cf. p. 65n[1].   [2] cf. p. 56.

but later, when the hour of Jesus' glory had come, they remembered how all this had been written of him beforehand, and how it had all come true.

So, the people who had been with Jesus when he called Lazarus from the tomb and restored him to life, testified to the truth of it all; and it was this same sign which caused the other crowd, when they heard tell of it, to come out of the city to meet him.

The pharisees, observing this, said one to another:

You see? We are doing no good at all:

the whole world is going over to him.

Among those who had come up to worship during the festival there were some Greeks.[1] These came to Philip, the man from Bethsaida in Galilee, and asked him: Sir, could we speak with Jesus? Philip told Andrew of this; and together they went to tell Jesus.

Then Jesus said:

So is the hour come

for the Son of Man to be glorified.

I tell you truly:

a grain of wheat,

unless it is put into the soil and dies,

remains just a grain;

but if it dies

it brings forth a rich harvest.

[1] cf. p. 84.

The man who loves his life
  as a miser his hoard,
    will lose it;
  the man who holds his life
  of little account in this world
    will keep for ever
      the life which is eternal.
Any man who would be my servant
  must follow me always:
    then, when I am come into the glory of my Father
    he will be with me still
    and my Father will honour him for serving me
      by giving him to share in the glory.

But now my soul is troubled.
  Yet what am I to say?
    Am I to beg my Father
      to save me from this my hour?
  It was for this hour that I came;
    in this the work given me is fulfilled
      and the glory of God's love made known.
  My prayer must be:
  Father, make known your glory.[1]
A voice came from heaven:
  I have made known my glory.
  I will make it known yet more.
Some of the crowd, hearing this sound, said God had
given Jesus a sign through the voice of the thunder;
others, that an angel had spoken to him.

[1] cf. p. 86.

Jesus said:
  This voice spoke
    not for my sake
      but for yours.
  For now, at this moment,
    sentence is being passed on the world;
    now, at this moment,
      he who has lorded it over the world[1]
        is condemned to be cast down.
  And I,
    when I am lifted up,[2]
      will draw all men to myself.
He said this to show what kind of death he would die.

The crowd answered him:
  We have learnt from the scriptures
    that the Christ is to live and reign for ever,
    but you say the Son of Man must be lifted up:
    who then is this Son of Man?
Jesus told them:
  Only for a little while longer
    will the light shine in your midst.
  Finish your journey whilst you have the light with you;
    do not let darkness overtake you;
      for he who journeys in darkness
        cannot know where he is going.
  While you still have the light with you
    put your faith in the light:

[1] cf. p. 84.   [2] cf. pp. 26, 33.

so you will become children of the light
and will never walk in darkness.

When he had said these things Jesus left them and hid
himself from them.
They, in spite of all the signs he had worked in their
sight, did not believe in him.
Thus they fulfilled the words of the prophet Isaiah:
    Lord, what man has put faith in our message?
     What man has understood
      the manifesting of God's power
       and so found faith?
For they did not believe
    because they could not believe;
     as Isaiah also said:
      His words have but blinded their eyes,
      his words have but hardened their hearts,
       and so they cannot turn to me
       and be healed by me.
Here Isaiah was speaking of Jesus:
he had seen in vision the hour of his glory.

There were many, even among the rulers of the people,
who did put their faith in him, but they would not proclaim their faith openly because of the pharisees: they
were afraid of being cast out from the synagogue. They
prized the esteem of men more highly than the glory
given by God.
But Jesus cried out:

He who believes in me
  gives his faith not to me
    but to him who sent me.
He who sees me
  sees him who sent me.
I, the light, came into the world
  that those who believe in me
    should no longer live in darkness.
If a man hears my words
  but will not wholly put his faith in them
    and obey them,
it is not I who will condemn him:
      I came not to condemn the world
           but to save the world.
The man who spurns my words
  because he rejects my right to utter them
    already has a judge who will try him:
those same words of mine
  will be his judge
    on the last day.
For the words I have spoken
  were not of my coining:
my Father, who sent me, told me
  what words I should speak,
  what message I should make known;
and I know that the message he gave me
  brings to men that life which is eternal.
Therefore all the words I speak
  are the words my Father told me to speak.

8. *The Last Supper*

13   It was the eve of the pasch or passover.

Jesus knew the hour had come for him to pass from this world and go to the Father. He had loved those who were his own, those he was leaving behind him in the world; now he would prove to them how boundlessly he loved them.

They had sat down to supper together.

Already the devil had put it into the heart of Judas son of Simon of Kerioth to betray him.

Jesus knew well that the Father had put everything into his hands. He knew it was from God he had come, and to God he was now to return. Nevertheless he took on himself now the appearance and office of a slave. He rose from the table, laid aside his clothes, and taking a towel he put it about him; then he poured water into a basin and set himself to wash his disciples' feet and dry them with the towel.[1] So he came to Simon Peter; but at once Peter said to him:

    Lord, is it for you to wash my feet?

Jesus answered him:

    You do not understand what I am doing:

      later on you will understand.

Peter cried:

    No! Never shall you wash my feet.

[1] cf. pp. 87 *sqq.*

Jesus told him:

    If I do not,

      you can have no companionship with me,

        being in spirit so far from me.

Peter said:

    Then, Lord, if that is so,

      wash not only my feet

        but my hands too and my head.

Jesus answered:

    A man who has bathed has no need to wash:

      he is already wholly clean.

    What I am doing is not for a cleansing:

      you, my companions, are already wholly clean,[1]

        though indeed not all of you.

(These last words, that they were not all of them clean,
he said because he knew who would betray him.)

When he had washed their feet he put on his clothes and
sat down again at table.

Then he said to them:

    Do you understand now what I have been doing?

      You call me your Master and your Lord:

        you are right:

          that is what I am.

    If I then, your Lord and Master,

              have washed your feet,

    you must wash one another's feet.

    I have set you an example:

      now you must do as I have done.

[1] cf. *infra* 15³ and *supra* p. 91.

I tell you truly:
   no slave can be greater than his master,
   no messenger greater than him whose message he
                                       bears.
Happy shall you be if,
   understanding these things,
     you also practise them.

I am not speaking of all of you when I say this:
   I know who my chosen ones are.
But the scripture must be fulfilled which says:
   The man who shared my bread
     has risen up to strike me.
And this I tell you now, before it happens,
    that when it does happen you may believe
        that I AM.

After this, Jesus went on:
   I tell you truly:
   he who welcomes my messenger
     welcomes me;
   and he who welcomes me
     welcomes him whose messenger I am.
But then, having said only this, he became deeply
troubled; and he made known his distress to them, saying:
   I tell you truly:
     one of you is going to betray me.
The disciples looked at one another, wondering whom he
meant. One of them, the disciple whom Jesus loved, was
reclining at table next to Jesus, his head close to Jesus'

breast. Simon Peter, beckoning to him, bade him ask which of them it was. So, leaning back on Jesus' breast, he murmured: Lord, who is it? Jesus answered: The one to whom I give this morsel I am dipping in the dish. And having dipped the morsel in the dish he gave it to Judas son of Simon of Kerioth. Judas took it; and immediately Satan entered into him.

Jesus said to him: What you are to do, do quickly.

None of those at table understood why he said this. As Judas kept the common purse, some thought Jesus was telling him to go and buy what was needed for the feast, or else to take an alms to the poor.

Judas, as soon as he had eaten the morsel, went out.

And it was night.[1]

9. *The Last Discourse*

When he had gone Jesus said:
  Now is the Son of Man glorified
   and God is glorified in him.
  And if his glory gives glory to God,
   so God in return will give him
    the glory which is his,
     and will give it soon.
  My children,
   only a little while longer now
    shall I be with you:

[1] cf. pp. 13, 27, 40.

you will look for me,
  but where I am going
  you cannot come.
I said this once to the Jews:
  I say it now to you.

But before I go away from you
  I give you a new commandment:[1]
  Love one another.
    Love one another
    as I have loved you.
  This is what will prove to all men
    you are my disciples:
    your love one for another.
Simon Peter asked him:
  Lord, where are you going?
Jesus answered:
  I am going where you cannot follow me now:
  later on you shall follow me.
Peter said:
  Lord, why cannot I follow you now?
  I am ready now to give my life for you.[2]
Jesus answered:
  You are ready to give your life for me?
  I tell you truly:
  before cock-crow
    you will have thrice disowned me.[3]

[1] cf. pp. 92–3.   [2] cf. p. 93.   [3] cf. p. 40.

14 Then Jesus said to them all:

Do not let your hearts be troubled.

You have faith in God:

have faith in me also.

In my Father's house many may dwell,

there is room for many;

else how could I have told you

I was going to prepare a home for you?

I am indeed going to prepare a home for you;

and then I shall come back for you

and take you home with me,

that where I am

you also may be.

And you know the way

that leads where I am going.

Thomas said to him:

But, Lord, we do not know where you are going:

how can we know the way that leads there?

Jesus answered:

I AM the way.[1]

I AM truth.

I AM life.

No one can go to the Father except by way of me.

If you have come to know me

you will know my Father also.

You do know him already:

you have seen him.

Philip said:

Lord, if you show us the Father

[1] cf. pp. 49 *sqq.*

there is nothing more we could ask.
Jesus answered him:
Philip, all this time I have been with you
and still you do not know me?
He who has seen me
has seen the Father;
so how can you say to me,
Show us the Father?
Do you not believe
that I live in the Father
and the Father lives in me?

The words I speak to you
are not of my coining:
they are given me by my Father.
And in the works I do it is my Father,
living in me,
who accomplishes his work.
Believe me then when I tell you
I live in the Father
and the Father lives in me.
Or, if you cannot believe because of
my words,
at least believe because of
the work:
I tell you truly:
he who has faith in me
will do the works I do,
and works yet greater will he do;

for now, my work accomplished,
  I am going to my Father and to my glory
    and so the Spirit will be given you:
    and whatever you ask,
      as my children,[1]
        I will grant it you,
  that the Father may be glorified
  in the Son;
    so, whatever you ask of me
      as my children
        I will do it.

If you love me
  you will obey the commands I give you;
then I will ask the Father
and he will give you another to befriend you
                        and defend you,[2]
    and to be with you always:
      the Spirit,
      the giver of truth.
The world will not accept the Spirit:
  it cannot see him
    and so will not recognize him.
But you know him

[1] lit. 'in my name'; the phrase as used here seems to mean simultaneously 'as my disciples', 'in union with me', and 'as appealing to my power and authority' (cf. e.g. Braun, *Evang.s.S.Jean*, in 14[13]); the above rendering is an attempt to convey this complex attitude of childlike dependence, trust and intimate family unity.
[2] cf. pp. 93–4.

because he lives with you
and within you.

I will not leave you friendless, orphaned:
soon I shall come back to you.
A little while now and the world will see me no more;
but you will see me
for I have life in me
and you too will have life in me
and sight of me;
and on that day, when I come back to you,
you will grasp what I mean
when I tell you now:
I live in my Father
and you live in me
and I in you.

He who knows in his heart
the meaning of my commands
and obeys them
truly loves me;
and he who loves me will be loved by my Father,
and I too will love him
and reveal myself to him.
Judas (not the Judas from Kerioth) said to him:
But, Lord, how is it you will reveal yourself
only to us,
not to the whole world?

Jesus answered:
    Because only he who loves me
      and therefore is true to the word I bring
              from my Father
    will be loved by my Father.
     To him we shall come,
    and shall live with him always.
  But for the man who does not love me
    this cannot be:
not loving me, he is not true to the word I bring,
    and that word is not of my coining
      but is the word of my Father
          who sent me.

This much have I told you
    while I am still with you:
later, when the holy Spirit comes to you—
    he who is to befriend and inspire you,
    he whom the Father will send you
              to speak in my name—
he will make everything plain to you
    and recall to your minds
      everything I have told you.

And now I bequeath you my peace:[1]
  I give you,
    not the peace the world understands
     and has to give,

[1] cf. p. 30.

but my peace
  which will not allow distress to overcome you
    or to make you play the coward
  but will keep you always in good heart.
You heard me say I am going from you now
  but will come back to you:
if you truly loved me
  you would be glad I am going to the Father,
    for the Father is greater than I.

All this I have told you before it takes place,
  that when it does take place
    you may be faithful.
I have little time left to me now
  to talk with you:
he who lords it over this world is at hand.
He has no hold over me,
  but what he is coming to do he must do:
so the world will learn that I love the Father
  and do as the Father bids me.

15   I AM the true vine
      and my Father is the vinegrower.
    Every barren branch of the vine
      he cuts away;
    every fruitful branch
      he trims clean
        to make it yet more fruitful.
    You, because of the words I have spoken to you,

the words which are life for you,
  are clean already;
but you must live always in me,
            and I in you:
for as the branch cannot bear fruit
  if it is cut off from the vine,
so you cannot bear fruit
  if you are cut off from me.

I AM the vine,
  you are my branches:
therefore apart from me you can do nothing.
If a man lives in me, and I in him,
  he will bear abundant fruit.
A man who does not live in me
  is like the branch that is cut off:
    it withers away
      and then is picked up
        and thrown into the fire
          and burnt.
As long as you live in me
  and my words live in you
    you may ask what you will
      and it will be granted you.
If you do bear abundant fruit
  you prove yourselves my disciples
    and then my Father is glorified.
      As the Father has loved me
        so I have loved you:

live, then, in my love.
And you will live in my love
if you obey the commands
I have given you,
just as I live in my Father's love
because I have obeyed
the commands he gave me.
All this I tell you
that my joy may be in your hearts
and your hearts may be brimful of joy.

This is the command I give you:
love one another as I have loved you.
There is no greater proof of love
than for a man to give his life
for the friends he loves.
You are my friends
if you do as I command you.
I shall not call you servants any more:
a servant does not know
what his master is about;
I call you my friends
because all that my Father has told me
I have made known to you.
It was not you who chose me:
I chose you,
chose you and appointed you
to be my messengers.
So you shall go out and bear fruit,
enduring fruit,

and whatever you ask of the Father,
  as my children,
he will give it to you.
All the demands I make of you are in this:
  that you love one another.
    If you find the world hates you—
      and you will—
    remember it hated me
      before it learned to hate you.
    If you belonged to the world
      it would recognize you for its own
        and would love you;
      but you do not belong to the world.
By choosing you I took you away from the world:
  that is why it hates you.
Remember too how I told you:
  the servant is not greater than his master.
    They will hound you
      as they have hounded me.
    They will pay as much heed to your words
      as they have to mine.
And they will do this to you because
  you represent me
and they cannot, in seeing me,
  see him who sent me.
If I had not come to them
  and spoken plainly to them
    they would not be guilty of sin;
as it is, their sin is without excuse.
He who hates me

hates my Father who sent me.
Had they not seen me do such works
 as no man else has done
  they would not be guilty of sin;
but they did see,
 and yet have hated
  both me and my Father.
So they fulfil those words of the scriptures:
 They have hated me without cause.

Later, another will bear witness to me:
 he who is to befriend and inspire you,
  the truth-giving Spirit
 who comes to you from the Father,
  whom I myself will send you
   from my Father's side.
So you too will bear witness to me,
 you who have been with me
  from the beginning.

16 I tell you all this now,
 that when trials come upon you
  your faith in me may stand unshaken.
They will thrust you out from their synagogues;
 more, the hour is now coming
  when those who kill you
   will claim to be serving God.
These things they will do

because they know neither the Father
            nor me.

I tell you this now,
  that when that hour comes
    you may remember I told you of it.
I did not tell you before:
  as long as I was with you
    there was no need.
But now I am going back to him who sent me.
  And none of you asks me, now,
    where I am going:
  your hearts are too full of sorrow
            at my going.
Yet I tell you truly:
  it is a good thing for you
    that I am going away from you,
      for if I do not go
he who is to befriend you will not come to you,
        but if I go
    I will send him to you.
And when he comes—
                to befriend you,
                to defend you—
he will expose the world's guilt
  in terms of sin, and justice, and judgement.
He will prove the world guilty of sin
  in that it refuses to have faith in me.
He will prove the justice of my claims
  by the fact that I am going to the Father

(and so you will see me no more).
He will show how, through my going,
  judgement is passed,
    not on me,
  but on him who till now
    has lorded it over the world.

Many more things I have to tell you,
  but as yet they are beyond your grasp.
When the truth-giving Spirit comes to you
  he will show you the fullness of the truth.
He will not give you words of his own coining:
  he will tell you what he himself will be told,
    showing you the unfolding
      of the new order of things.
In doing this he will give glory to me;
  for what he imparts to you
    he will have received from me.
And I say he will have received it from me
  because all that belongs to the Father
                belongs to me.
In a little while you will see me no longer;
  but then, a little while after that,
    you will see me again.

At this some of the disciples said one to another:
  What can this little while mean,
    after which we see him no longer
      yet then we see him again?
  And did he not say he is going back to the Father?

What can he mean?
Jesus, knowing they wanted to question him, said to
them:
You are wondering what these words mean.
I tell you truly:
for a time you will be sad, and weep,
because of my going,
while the world rejoices
to be rid of me;
for a time your hearts will be full of grief,
but then your grief will be turned into joy.
A woman in childbirth knows the pangs of childbirth;
but when she has borne her child
her pangs are forgotten
in the joy of bringing a man into the world.
So you too are sad for a time;
but I shall see you again
and then your hearts will be glad
with a gladness no man can take from you.
In that day you will no longer need to question me;
but you will need to pray;
and I tell you truly,
whatever you ask of my Father,
as my children,
he will grant it you for my sake.
Till now, because I have been with you,
you have not asked anything of him
for my sake;
but when I am with the Father, ask,
and what you ask he will give you.

And in this closeness to him
  your joy will be complete.

I speak to you of these things at present
  in veiled words;[1]
but the hour is coming when I shall speak to you
  through the Spirit,
    not in veiled words but openly,
      about my Father.
And you will not need me then
  to intercede for you:
you have believed that I came from God,
you have loved me,
    therefore my Father will love you
                  and will hear your prayer.
I did indeed come from the Father
  into this world;
now I am leaving this world
  and going to the Father.

At this his disciples said:
  Now you are indeed speaking
    not in veiled words but openly.
  Now we can see you know all things:
    you know the questions we would ask you
    without our asking them.
  Now therefore we do indeed believe
              you came from God.

[1] cf. p. 31.

Jesus answered:
  You really have faith in me now?
   Yet the hour is coming—
    is indeed already come—
   when you will all be scattered,
    each of you going his own way,
     and will leave me quite alone.
   (Yet I can never be alone:
    always the Father is with me.)
   I have told you all these things
    that in me you may find peace.
   In the world you will find suffering;
    but be of good heart:
    I have conquered the world.

7 Thus Jesus spoke.
  Then, lifting up his eyes to heaven, he said:
   Father, the hour has come.
   Give glory now to your Son
    that your Son may thereby
     give glory to you,
   just as you have given him authority
    over all mankind
   that he may bestow the life which is eternal
    on all those you have given him.
        And this is life eternal:
         to know, lovingly,
          and to glorify
        you, the only true God,
        and him whom you sent,

God's messenger,
man's Messiah,
Jesus.

I have given glory to you on earth
  by finishing the work you gave me to do.
Do you now, Father, make me glorious at your side
  with that glory which was mine
    before the world was made and time began.

I have made you known
  to those you chose out from the world
    and entrusted to me.
They belonged to you from the beginning
  but you gave them to me that I might teach them
    and they have kept and carried out your word.
They know now that all you have given me
  does come only from you.
    The words you entrusted to me
      I have entrusted to them
        and they have accepted them.
So they have seen that in truth I came from you;
  they have believed it was you who sent me.

For these then I pray,
  not for the world
    but for these you have given me;
      for they belong to you,

and as all that belongs to me is yours
so all that belongs to you is mine.

For these I pray
  because through them and in them now
    my glory is to shine forth.
For these I pray
  because now I am going to you
    and shall be no more in the world,
      but these whom I leave behind
        will be in the world.

        Holy Father,
      keep them loyal to you,
    to that revealing of your holiness
which you gave me to make known to them,
      that they may be one
        as we are one.

While I have been with them
  I have kept them loyal to you.
  I have watched over them
    so that none of them has been lost,
      none but him who chose to be lost[1]

[1] lit. 'son of perdition': as the Jerusalem Bible notes, this semitism means one doomed to perdition 'without however implying any denial of his responsibility'; cp. Braun (*op. cit.*): 'John tells us it is through his own fault that Judas goes to his doom'. Cf. *supra*, p. 70, for a discussion of the general principle that to be condemned is to be self-condemned.

and so fulfilled
what the scriptures foretold.
But now I am coming to you
and so I speak these words
while I am yet with them
that they may have my own joy in their hearts,
filling their hearts brimful.

I have made known to them your word
and they have received it;
and so the world hates them
since they do not belong to the world
just as I do not belong to the world.
But I do not ask you
to take them out of the world:
only to guard them
from the Evil in the world.
They are not of the world,
just as I am not of the world,
but they must work in the world.
Do you, then, make them holy
by means of the truth:
the truth that penetrates and transforms,
the truth that is your word.
For as you dedicated me
and sent me into the world,
so I have dedicated them
and sent them into the world;
and now I dedicate myself, a victim, for them
that they also may be truly dedicated.

But I do not pray only for them:
  I pray also for those
    who will be led by their words
      to put their faith in me:
  I pray that they may all be one.
  I pray, Father, that as you live in me
                      and I live in you
    so they may live in us.
So shall the world learn to believe
  in your sending of me to the world.

And I have given them
  the splendour of life you gave me
that they may be one as we are one,
        I living in them,
        you living in me,
that their unity may be perfect and complete.
    So shall the world know
      that you sent me
and that you did so because you loved them
      as you loved me.

Father:
  all those you have given me
    I would have to be with me
      where I am soon to be
that they may be gladdened by seeing my glory,
  that glory which you have given me
    because of the love you bore me
    before the world was made and time began.

Father, you are just:
the world will not acknowledge you
but I acknowledge you
and these have acknowledged that you sent me:
so I have made you known to them
and will make you known to them yet more,
that the love you have borne me
may live in them
and I may live in them too.

10. Passion and Glory

18 After this, Jesus said to his disciples:
Come, we must be on our way.
So they went out, and crossed over the brook called
Kedron, or Dark Torrent.[1] There was, on the other side,
a garden;[2] and into this they went. Judas, the betrayer,
knew the place well, for Jesus had often gone there with
his disciples. So now he came, bringing with him a detach-
ment of Roman soldiers, and guards sent by the chief
priests and pharisees, with lanterns and torches and
weapons.
Jesus, knowing all that was to happen to him, went out to
them and asked them:
Who is it you seek?
They answered:
Jesus of Nazareth.

[1] cf. p. 94.   [2] cf. p. 95.

He said to them:

    I AM he.[1]

Judas, who betrayed him, was standing amongst them.
When Jesus told them, I AM he, they shrank back and fell
to the ground.[2]

He asked them again:

    Who is it you seek?

Again they answered:

    Jesus of Nazareth.

Jesus said:

    I have told you already that I am he.

    If I am the one you are looking for

      let these others go free.

For he wanted to make good what he had said of those
who had been given him: that none of them had been lost.
Then Simon Peter, who had a sword, drew it and struck
the servant of the high priest, a man named Malchus, and
cut off his right ear.[3]

Jesus said to Peter:

    Sheathe your sword.

    Am I not to drink the cup

      my Father himself has given me?

Then the Roman officer and his men, and the Jewish
guards, seized Jesus and bound him. They led him first to
Annas, the father-in-law of Caiphas who held the office
of high priest in that year. But Annas ordered him to be
taken, still bound, before Caiphas. (It was Caiphas who
had counselled the Jews: Better that one man should die
for the sake of the people.)

    [1] cf. p. 33n.   [2] cf. p. 105n[4].   [3] cf. p. 30.

Simon Peter had followed Jesus, with another disciple who was known to the high priest. This disciple went in with Jesus into the high priest's court, while Peter remained at the door, outside. Presently the other disciple, who knew the high priest, went back and spoke to the maid-servant at the door, and so brought Peter in.

But the maid-servant said to Peter: Are not you also one of this man's disciples?

He answered: I am not.

It was cold; the servants and guards had made a charcoal fire and were standing by it, warming themselves. So Peter stood there with them, warming himself like the others.

The high priest now questioned Jesus about his disciples and his teaching.

Jesus said to him:

    I have spoken openly before the world.

    I have taught in the synagogues and in the temple
       where all the Jews assemble.

    I have said nothing in secret.

     Why then do you question me?

    Ask those who listened to me what I taught them:
       they know what I said.

At this, one of the guards, who was standing close by Jesus, slapped his face,[1] saying:

    Is that how you answer the high priest?

Jesus said to him:

    If I spoke wrongly, point out the wrong;

[1] cf. p. 107.

if not, why do you strike me?

Meanwhile, as Simon Peter stood warming himself, they said to him:

Are not you also one of his disciples?

He denied it, saying:

No, I am not.

One of the high priest's servants, a kinsman of the man whose ear Peter had cut off, said:

Surely I saw you with him in the garden?

Peter again denied it.

Immediately, a cock crew.[1]

And now they led Jesus from Caiphas' house to the governor's palace.

It was early morning.

They would not go into the palace themselves: by their traditions, to enter a pagan's house is to incur legal defilement, and they wanted to eat the paschal meal. So Pilate came out to them.

He asked them:

What charge do you bring against this man?

They answered:

If he were not an evil-doer
we should not have brought him before you.

Pilate said:

Take him then and judge him yourselves
according to your own law.

But the Jews answered:

[1] cf. p. 40.

We are not allowed to put anyone to death.

(In saying this they carried forward the fulfilment of what Jesus had said concerning the kind of death he would die.)[1]

Pilate went back into the palace, and had Jesus brought before him.

He asked him:

You are the king of the Jews?

Jesus said:

Is that your own question

or do you ask it

because of what others have said of me?

Pilate answered:

Am I a Jew?

It is your own nation,

your own chief priests,

who have given you up to me.

What is it you have done?

Jesus answered:

My kingship is not of the kind this world can bestow.

Had I wanted to be a king of that kind

my followers would have fought

to save me from the clutches of the Jews;

but my kingship is not of that kind.

Pilate said:

But you are, nevertheless, a king?

Jesus answered:

[1] Had Jesus been the victim of mob-violence or been put to death (illegally) by order of the Sanhedrin he would have been stoned; the recourse to Pilate in fact ensured that he would die by being lifted up on the cross.

I am a king.
But this is what my kingship means:
  I was born,
  I came into the world,
    to bear witness to the truth,
  and whoever has the truth in him
    will listen to my voice:
  so the truth will make him free,
    the truth will make him a king
      through sharing in my kingship.[1]
Pilate shrugged and said:
  What is truth?
Then he went out again to the Jews, and said to them:
  I see no reason why I should condemn this man.
  And it is your custom to ask me, at the passover,
    to release a prisoner:
  shall I then release the king of the Jews?
They cried out:
  No, not this man:
    release Barabbas.
(Barabbas was a robber.)

9 Pilate then gave orders that Jesus should be flogged.[2] The soldiers, when they had done this, amused themselves by plaiting a crown of thorns and putting it on his head, and dressing him in a scarlet cloak;[3] then, coming up to him, they would cry, Hail, king of the Jews! and slap his face.

Presently Pilate went back to the Jews and said to them:

    [1] cf. p. 17.   [2] cf. p. 96.   [3] cf. pp. 87, 96.

I am going to bring him out to you now,
  and you will see I cannot take his case seriously.
Jesus came out, wearing the crown of thorns and the scarlet cloak.
Pilate said to them:
  Here is the man.[1]
But when the chief priests and their guards saw him they shouted:
  To the cross with him! To the cross!
Pilate said:
  Take him yourselves, then, to the cross:
  I see no reason to condemn him.
The Jews retorted:
  We have a law,
    and according to that law he must die:
    he made himself out to be the Son of God.
When Pilate heard this he went back into the palace. He was very afraid.[2]
He said to Jesus:
  What are you? Where have you come from?[3]
Jesus made no reply.[4]
Then Pilate said:
  You refuse to speak to me?
  Do you not know I have power
    either to set you free
    or to crucify you?

---

[1] cf. p. 110.   [2] cf. p. 105.
[3] cf. p. 105n3.   [4] cf. pp. 56, 105.

Jesus answered:

> You would have no power over me at all
> had it not been given you from above.
> But you are troubled
> at the thought of abusing your power:
> therefore he who gave me up to you
> is more guilty than you.

Because of this, Pilate became yet more anxious to find a way of setting Jesus free.

But the Jews shouted:

> If you set this man free
> you cannot be Caesar's friend:
> any man who makes himself king
> is Caesar's rival.

When he heard this, Pilate had Jesus brought out again. He sat down in his judgement seat, to pronounce official sentence, in the place called Lithostrotos, which means a paved place; the Hebrew name is Gabbatha.

It was now about noon,[1] on the eve of the paschal feast.

Pilate said to the Jews:

> Here is your king.

They cried out:

> Away with him! Away with him! Crucify him!

Pilate said:

> Am I to crucify your king?

[1] cf. pp. 62, 100.

The chief priests answered:

We have no king but Caesar.

Then at last Pilate gave Jesus up to them, to be crucified. They led him away.

And carrying his cross[1] he went out of the city to the place called Golgotha, which means The Place of the Skull.[2] There they crucified him, with two others, one on each side of him and Jesus in the middle.

Pilate had ordered this inscription to be written out and fixed to the cross:

Jesus of Nazareth, the king of the Jews.

This was read by many Jews, for the place where Jesus was crucified is close to the city and the inscription was written in Hebrew, Latin and Greek; so the chief priests went to Pilate and protested:

You should not write, The king of the Jews;

you should write,

This man said he was the king of the Jews.

Pilate answered:

What I have written stands.

The soldiers, when they had crucified Jesus, gathered up his clothes to divide them into four portions, one for each of them. But the tunic was seamless, woven all of a piece; so they said:

Let us not cut this up, but cast lots for it.

So the words of the scripture were fulfilled:

They shared out my clothing among them,

[1] cf. pp. 56, 107n.   [2] cf. pp. 107–8.

they cast lots for my robe.

In this way the soldiers occupied themselves. But close beside the cross of Jesus were his mother, and her sister, and Mary the wife of Cleophas, and Mary of Magdala. Jesus, seeing his mother and, standing near her, the disciple he loved, said first to his mother:

Woman, that is your son.[1]

Then he said to the disciple:

That is your mother.

And from that hour the disciple took her into his own keeping and his own home.

Then Jesus, knowing that all had now been accomplished, said:

I am thirsty.

And so his fulfilling of the scriptures was also brought to completion.[2]

A jar was standing there full of vinegar:[3] they filled a sponge with the vinegar and, fixing it to a bunch of hyssop,[4] lifted it to his mouth.

[1] cf. p. 108.

[2] cf. *Ps.* 68[22]: 'They gave me gall for my food, and in my thirst they gave me vinegar to drink.'

[3] cf. pp. 96, 107.

[4] Scholars suggest that *hyssōpō* is a copyist's mistake for *hyssō* (i.e. a lance, the *pilum* of the legionaries) which matches the *kalamos* (reed) of the synoptists and avoids the obvious difficulty that hyssop would be too fragile to support the weight of the sponge. But (like the 'children' in *Daniel*, mentioned above) the hyssop is symbolically very apt: it reminds us of the O.T. purification-rituals (e.g. *Levit.* 14[4]) and above all of the paschal lamb and blood-sprinklings of

Jesus drank the vinegar.

Then he said:

The work is done.[1]

And he let his head sink down as though to sleep,[2]
and yielded up his spirit.

The Jews did not want the bodies to remain on the crosses during the sabbath, for this sabbath was a solemn one. So, as it was now the eve, they asked Pilate to order that their legs be broken, to hasten death: then the bodies could be taken away. Pilate accordingly sent soldiers. They broke the legs of the two who had been crucified with Jesus; but when they came to Jesus himself they found him already dead, so they did not break his legs but one of them pierced his side with a lance,[3] and immediately there flowed out blood and water.[4]

He who saw this bears witness to it, and his testimony is worthy of trust. He tells what he knows to be true, that you, like him, may believe. For this was done in fulfilment of the words of the scriptures:

Not one of his bones shall be broken;

and again:

They shall look on him whom they pierced.[5]

After this, Joseph of Arimathea, who had been a disciple of Jesus though in secret because he feared the Jews,

[1] cf. p. 27n[1].   [2] cf. p. 60.   [3] cf. pp. 28–30, 48.
[4] cf. p. 13.   [5] cf. p. 28.

Exodus 12[22], and, in christian ritual, of the symbolism of the _Asperges_ (_Ps._ 50[9]) and of the baptismal waters in general.

asked Pilate to allow him to take away the body of Jesus.
Pilate gave leave. So he came to take the body; and
Nicodemus, the man who had visited Jesus by night,
came also, bringing a mixture of myrrh and aloes of about
a hundred pounds' weight. They took Jesus' body, and
wrapped it in winding-bands with the aromatic spices
according to the Jewish custom of burying their dead.
There was a garden in the place where Jesus had been
crucified, and in the garden a new tomb in which no one
had as yet been laid. Here then, since it was close at hand
and there was little time before the feast on the morrow,
they buried Jesus.

On the morning of the first day of the week, very early,
while it was still dark,[1] Mary of Magdala made her way
to the tomb. And she found that the stone had been
moved away from the entrance.
So she ran to find Simon Peter, and the other disciple
also, the one Jesus loved; and she told them: They have
carried the Lord away from the tomb, and we do not
know where they have taken him.
At once Peter set out, with the other disciple, and they
began running together to the tomb. But the other disciple, being the more speedy, outran Peter and reached it
first. Bending down,[2] and glancing into the tomb, he saw
the winding-bands lying on the ground; but he did not
go in.
Simon Peter then came up, and went into the tomb. He
too saw the winding-bands lying there; and also the cloth

[1] cf. p. 23.   [2] cf. p. 54.

which had covered Jesus' head: this was not with the
rest of the linen but was lying rolled up in a separate
place.

The other disciple, who had reached the tomb first, then
went in also.

He saw; and he believed.

(For until now they still had not understood how the
scriptures showed that Jesus was to rise from the dead.)

The disciples then returned home.

But Mary stayed close by the tomb, outside the entrance,
weeping. And as she wept she bent down and looked into
the tomb. And she saw two angels clothed in white sitting
in the place where Jesus' body had lain, one at the head,
the other at the feet.

They said to her:

    Why are you weeping?

She answered:

    They have carried away my Lord

      and I do not know where they have taken him.

As she said this she turned round and saw Jesus standing
there; but she did not realize it was he.

Jesus asked her:

    Why are you weeping?

    Who is it you are seeking?

She, thinking him to be the gardener, said to him:

    Sir, if it was you who carried him from here,

      tell me where you have laid him

      that I may go and take him away.

Jesus said to her:

    Mary.

Then she turned again to him,[1] and said to him:

Rabbouni (that is, My Master).

Jesus said to her:

You must not cling to me:[2]

I have not yet ascended to my Father,

though very soon now I am to do so.

No, go and find my brethren

and tell them what I have just told you:

that I am to go to him who is my Father and your

Father,

my God and your God.

So Mary of Magdala went to the disciples with her message.

She said to them:

I have seen the Lord.

And she told them what he had said.

Late in the evening of that same day, the first day of the week, the disciples were gathered together. For fear of the Jews they had locked the doors of the room where they were. Then, of a sudden, Jesus was standing in the midst of them.

He said to them:

Peace to you.

And he showed them his hands and his side.

Thus the disciples saw the Lord again; and were filled with joy.

He said to them again:

Peace to you.

[1] cf. p. 98.   [2] cf. pp. 114–15.

As the Father sent me,
so now I send you.
And he breathed upon them, and said to them:
Receive the power of the holy Spirit:[1]
when you forgive men their sins
they shall in truth be forgiven;
when you hold them bound
they shall in truth be bound.

When this took place, one of the twelve, Thomas (that is to say, The Twin), was not present with the rest.[2]
The other disciples told him:
We have seen the Lord.
He said to them:
Unless I see in his hands
the marks of the nails,
unless I put my finger in the place
where the nails were,
and my hand into his side,
I will not believe.

Eight days later the disciples were again gathered together behind locked doors; and this time Thomas was with them.
Jesus came as before and stood in the midst of them, and said to them:
Peace to you.
Then he said to Thomas:
Give me your finger:

[1] cf. p. 116.   [2] cf. p. 116.

look, here are my hands.
Give me your hand:
now, put it into my side.
And be a doubter no longer
but give me your faith.
Thomas said to him:
My Lord and my God.
Jesus said:
Because you have seen me you believe?
Happy are they who, not having seen me,
give me their faith.

Later, Jesus showed himself again to the disciples.[1] It was by the sea of Tiberias. This is what happened. Simon Peter, Thomas or The Twin, Nathanael of Cana in Galilee, the sons of Zebedee, and two more of his disciples were all together there.
Simon Peter told them:
I am going out fishing.
They said:
We will go with you.
So they all went out, and got into the boat. But throughout that night they caught nothing.
Dawn came; and there was Jesus, standing on the seashore; but they did not know it was he.
He called out to them:
Have you caught anything, men?[2]
They answered:
No.

[1] cf. pp. 117 *sqq.*   [2] cf. p. 118n.

He said:

> Cast the net to the right of the boat
> and you will have a catch.

They did as he said; and before long they found they could not haul in the net, so great was their catch of fish. Then the disciple whom Jesus loved said to Peter:

> It is the Lord.

Simon Peter, hearing this, tied his coat about him, for he had been naked,[1] and threw himself into the water. The other disciples followed in the boat—they were not far from land, only a hundred yards or so—dragging their catch behind them. When they had come ashore they found a charcoal fire burning there, with fish cooking on it, and bread.

Jesus said to them:

> Bring some of the fish you have caught.

Simon Peter, going on board, hauled the net ashore. It was full of great fish, a hundred and fifty-three of them.[2] But for all that it did not break.

Jesus said to them:

> Come, eat.

None of the disciples could bring himself to ask, Who are you? In their hearts they knew it was the Lord. Jesus, taking the bread, brought it to each of them, and the fish as well.

So for the third time he showed himself to his disciples after his rising from the dead.

When the meal was over, Jesus said to Simon Peter:

[1] cf. p. 90.   [2] cf. p. 118.

244

Simon son of John,
   do you love me more than these others?[1]
He answered:
   Yes, Lord, you know I love you.
Jesus said to him:
   Then you must feed my lambs.
Again a second time he asked him:
   Simon son of John, do you love me?
He answered:
   Yes, Lord, you know I love you.
Yet a third time he asked him:
   Simon son of John, do you love me?
Peter was distressed at being asked yet a third time.
   Lord, he said,
      you know all things:
         you know well,
         you can see,
            that I love you.
Then Jesus said to him:
   You must feed my sheep.
   I tell you truly:
      when you were young
         you would tie your belt about you
            and set out
               for wherever you felt minded to go;
      when you are grown old
         you will hold out your arms
         to let another tie your belt about you
            and lead you

[1] cf. p. 115.

where you are not minded to go.[1]
Jesus said this to show Peter the kind of death by which
he was to glorify God.

And so he ended by saying:

Follow me.[2]

Then, as he began to move away, Peter followed after
him. But hearing another following them he turned
round and saw it was the disciple whom Jesus loved. This
was the one who at the supper had leaned back on Jesus'
breast and asked him who would betray him.

So Peter said to Jesus:

And this one, Lord: what of him?

Jesus answered:

Suppose I should want him to remain
   until I come again:
   what is that to you?
What you have to do is
   to follow me.

It was this that gave rise to the idea among the brethren
that this disciple was not to die. But Jesus did not say he
was not to die. He said only: Suppose I should want him
to remain until I come, what is that to you?

It is that same disciple who bears witness to all these
events and has set down this account of them; and we
know that his witness is worthy of trust.

Many other signs Jesus worked
in the presence of his disciples

[1] cf. p. 115.   [2] cf. p. 102.

which are not recounted here.
If all the things Jesus did were written down
the whole world would not, I think, contain
the books they would fill.
This much has been written
that you may believe fully and firmly
that Jesus is the Christ
and the Son of God
and so believing
may, in him, have
LIFE.

ST. JOSEPH'S NOVITIATE
BAILEYS HARBOR, WISCONSIN

STATE
BRANCH ____ WISCONSIN